Practice Test #1

Practice Questions

English

Numbers 1-15 pertain to the following passage:

The Wampanoag Indians of the Northeast were typical of the tribes of the time. They (1)speak a language that is a part of the Algonquin language family. At that time, the Wampanoag people lived (2)in what is Massachusetts. (3)Today, the descendants of these Indians speak English and live in southern Massachusetts and Rhode Island.

The Wampanoag religion was similar to that of the other Algonquin tribes. In those bygone times, the people believed in a Great Spirit (4)and also that all things in Nature had a part of the Great Spirit in them. They also had spiritual beliefs (5)about animals, and the forest. They expressed their religious beliefs during festivals and at night, when they sat together at huge campfires. Then, they told (6)their stories of the cycle of life (7)and the Great Spirit. Now, (8)some Indians that are a part of the Wampanoags still worship in the traditional (9)way but many have adopted western religions.

The Wampanoag diet consisted mostly of fish and other (10)animals, they also ate (11)corn, and beans, and squash. The Wampanoag hunters ranged far and wide, from land to (12)the sea. They trapped small animals and caught shellfish, including crabs and lobsters. (13)Besides animals, they grew fruits and vegetables. To survive the winter, they were able to preserve a lot of this food (14)and eat it.

The Wampanoag lived in houses (15)called a *wetu*. A *wetu* is a round building with a round roof. The men of the tribe were responsible for constructing the *wetu*. They made thedwelling by tying sticks and branches together, and then putting grass and tree bark on top to make the roof. The Wampanoag also built long houses, which were much larger and were used for tribal meetings.

1. A. no change
   B. spoke
   C. understand
   D. speaks

2. F. no change
   G. in what is now Massachusetts
   H. in
   J. in Massachusetts now

3. A. no change
    B.Recent descendants
    C.Today the descendants
    D.Current descendants

4. F.and, also
    G.and
    H.also
    J.no change

5. A. no change
    B. about animals, and about the
    C. about animals and the
    D. and the

6. F. no change
    G. there
    H. they're
    J. sitting

7. A. no change
    B. of the
    C. and of the
    D. and, of the

8. F. no change
    G. some Wampanoags
    H. some Indians
    J. some Indians that are Wampanoags

9. A. no change
    B. way, but many
    C. way, but, many
    D. way, many

10. F. no change
    G. animals, and they also
    H. animals, also
    J. animals. They also

11. A. no change
    B. corn, and beans and squash
    C. corn, beans, and squash
    D. corn beans and squash

12. F. no change
    G. near the
    H. over
    J. OMIT THIS WORD

13. A. no change
   B. Besides hunting
   C. Besides, hunting
   D. Other than animals,

14. F. no change
   G. OMIT THIS PHRASE
   H. while eating it
   J. while they ate it

15. A. no change
   B. called wetu
   C. or wetu
   D. in wetu

Numbers 16-30 pertain to the following passage:

In 2001, 34% of the population of the United States was overweight. Problems of excessive weight (16)<u>would seem to be</u> associated with the wealth and (17)<u>more than sufficient</u> food supply. (18)<u>Much attention in recent years has been paid</u> to physical fitness and (19)<u>changing their diets</u> to become healthier. It seems logical that, with so much emphasis on health and nutrition, (20)<u>that</u> the solution to our nation's obesity problem would be in (21)<u>sight</u>. However, in a study of a population with moderate food insecurity, it was found that (22)<u>52%</u> were overweight. *Food insecurity* exists when the availability of nutritionally adequate and safe foods or the ability to acquire acceptable foods in socially acceptable ways is limited or uncertain. Over half of (23)the <u>United State's</u>population with a threat of hunger is overweight. Why would obesity be more prevalent among this group of people who have *fewer* resources?

Dieting and surgery do not address the problems of the economic groups with the most severe weight and nutrition problems. Surgery is expensive, and people with limited resources are (24)<u>still</u> not likely to buy expensive health foods when there are cheaper alternatives that satisfy (25)<u>your</u> hunger. The dollar menu at a fast food restaurant is certainly less expensive than preparing a well-balanced meal, (26)<u>and easier too</u>. Another reason for obesity in lower income groups is given by (27)<u>a theory called</u> the paycheck cycle theory. Most paychecks are distributed on a monthly basis, so if a family gets a paycheck, (28)<u>the family</u> will use these resources until they run out. Often money can be depleted before the next distribution. When this happens, there is an involuntary restriction of food. The hypothesis suggests (29)<u>that a</u> cycle of food restriction at the end of the month followed by bingeing that would promote weight gain. The main reasons for obesity and overweight in low-income groups (30)<u>would be</u> periodic food restriction and a poor diet because of financial restrictions.

16. F. no change
   G. are
   H. seem to be
   J. are not

17. A. no change
    B. more, then sufficient
    C. more, than sufficient
    D. more-than-sufficient

18. F. no change
    G. In recent years, much attention has been paid
    H. Much attention, in recent years, has been paid
    J. In recent years much attention

19. A. no change
    B. diet
    C. changing diet there
    D. changing your diet

20. F. no change
    G. OMIT the word
    H. for
    J. when

21. A. no change
    B. site
    C. cyte
    D. cite

22. F. no change
    G. 52% of them
    H. 52% of the population
    J. 52% of it

23. A. no change
    B. United States's
    C. United States
    D. United State

24. F. no change
    G. OMIT word
    H. often
    J. frequently

25. A. no change
    B. OMIT word
    C. ones
    D. the

26. F. no change
    G. and easier to
    H. and easier two
    J. and easier, too

27. A. no change
    B. OMIT expression
    C. something called
    D. a hypothesis called

28. F. no change
    G. OMIT expression
    H. they
    J. someone

29. A. no change
    B. that
    C. that there is
    D. doing a

30. F. no change
    G. are
    H. seem to be
    J. come from

Numbers 31-45 pertain to the following passage:

Volta Hall is a (31)<u>womens</u> residence located at the western side of campus. It is composed of a (32)<u>porters</u> lodge, a small chapel, a dining hall, a library, a small laundry service, a hair salon, a small (33)<u>convenient</u> store, and three residential buildings designated for students.

Volta Hall has a total of three entry points that (34)<u>accesses</u> the entire structure. Two of these entries are located on the sides of the dining hall and are left unlocked and unprotected throughout the day. In the evening, usually (35)<u>some time</u> shortly after seven o'clock, these (36)<u>entryways</u> are locked by Volta Hall personnel. This leaves only the main entry, which is located at the front of the hall, (37)<u>as the only way</u> for individuals entering and exiting the hall. No record is kept of students or other persons entering and exiting the building. No identification is required to receive room keys from the porters. Security is so lax that students <u>(38)have been known to even receive</u> more than one room key from the porters and (39)<u>even</u> grab keys from behind the desk without giving notice.

The main entrance is guarded by two porters 24 hours (40)<u>out of each day</u>. The porters are most alert during the morning and early afternoon. During the evening <u>(41)hours</u> and early morning, the porters can be found sleeping. The main entry is usually closed during the late evening and reopened in the morning. Although these doors are closed, individuals have been known to open the latches from the outside, without forcing them, to gain entry.

There are usually additional security guards on the second level. During the day, two security guards are (42)<u>on watch or lack there of</u>. These guards are elderly men who have been known to respond to incidents very slowly, have poor eyesight, are unarmed, (43)<u>and physically out of shape</u>. Throughout the day and most of the evening, these guards can be found asleep at their post. Only one guard is on duty during the evening hours. These men can be found periodically walking around the perimeter of the building "checking" on students. These tactics have been (44)proven to be ineffective (45)toward criminal incidents occurring within the hall.

31. A. no change
    B. woman's
    C. women's
    D. womens's

32. F. no change
    G. porter
    H. porter's
    J. porters's

33. A. no change
    B. OMIT word
    C. convenience
    D. connivance

34. F. no change
    G. come into
    H. come in to
    J. provide access to

35. A. no change
    B. OMIT expression
    C. sometimes
    D. a little

36. F. no change
    G. entry ways
    H. door ways
    J. windows

37. A. no change
    B. OMIT phrase
    C. as the way
    D. as the best way

38. F. no change
    G. receive
    H. have even been known to receive
    J. get

39. A. no change
    B. OMIT word
    C. even to
    D. to

40. F. no change
    G. a day
    H. at a time
    J. on their shifts

41. A. no change
    B. OMIT word
    C. entrance
    D. hour's

42. F. no change
    G. on watch or lack thereof
    H. supposedly on watch
    J. not enough

43. A. no change
    B. and out of shape
    C. and are physically out of shape
    D. and are out of shape

44. F. no change
    G. OMIT expression
    H. proved to be
    J. tried to be

45. A. no change
    B. OMIT word
    C. when it comes to
    D. in curbing

Numbers 46-60 pertain to the following passage:

Student Log Entry:

This is the first log entry for Mountain Maritime High (46)<u>School's</u> "Student Sailors" program. Our high school mascot is a sea lion, so we call ourselves the "Mountain Lions." We are going out on a university research vessel to collect water from the bottom of the Straits of San Juan.

Our journey began as we cruised over to Victoria on a ferry after a long flight. We were glad that the school paid for all of our transportation because we would have had to (47)<u>have done</u> a lot of car washes to (48)<u>have afforded</u> this trip. (49)<u>At last, we finally</u> boarded our ship on Vancouver Island and got settled in our berths. Soon we met the captain and crew, and (50)<u>soon</u> we were on our way. We sailed for several (51)<u>hours until</u> we arrived at the underwater Axial Volcano on the San Juan Ridge.

When we arrived, the Chief (52)<u>Scientist Dr. Ed Cook and his crew</u> got ready to collect the water samples. Soon, they were ready to cast out (53)<u>this</u> bundle of sampling bottles. The bottles close at any depth so that water can (54)<u>bring</u> back up to the lab. (55)<u>So far we have learned that</u> they are testing the water for trace metals such as iron, manganese, and helium isotopes.

The Axial Volcano erupted in 1998, and these tests (56)<u>will be used to detect</u> what the scientists call magmatic activity . We spoke with a scientist who is filtering the water to find (57)<u>these</u> tiny specks called teps. She thinks they ride up on the hot water plume that moves up from the vents. (58)<u>Last night</u> we were amazed at the marine life that comes up from the depths to see the lights on the (59)<u>ship and all</u>. There are so many marine scientists aboard that we had no trouble finding out (60)<u>what the names are </u>of what we saw.

46. F. no change
    G. schools
    H. Schools
    J. school's

47. A. no change
    B. do
    C. did
    D. have

48. F. no change
    G. have paid for
    H. afford
    J. have done

49. A. no change
    B. At last, we
    C. Finally, at last we
    D. We at last

50. F. no change
    G. sooner
    H. then
    J. lately

51. A. no change
    B. hours, until
    C. hours and
    D. hours

52. F. no change
    G. Scientist Dr. Ed Cook, and his crew
    H. Scientist, Dr. Ed Cook and his crew
    J. Scientist, Dr. Ed Cook, and his crew

53. A. no change
    B. OMIT word
    C. a
    D. some

54. F. no change
   G. brang
   H. be brought
   J. be brung

55. A. no change
   B. OMIT phrase
   C. So far, we have learned that
   D. So far we have learned, that

56. F. no change
   G. will detect
   H. will look for
   J. will test for

57. A. no change
   B. OMIT word
   C. some
   D. any

58. F. no change
   G. Last night,
   H. START NEW PARAGRAPH
   J. OMIT phrase

59. A. no change
   B. ship, and all.
   C. ship, and everything
   D. ship.

60. F. no change
   G. what are the names
   H. the names
   J. what the names were

Numbers 61-75 pertain to the following passage:

Once upon a time, (61)<u>there was</u> a village in the jungle, a man appeared and announced to the villagers that he would buy monkeys for $10 each.

(62)<u>Seeing as how</u> there were many monkeys around, the villagers went out to the (63)<u>forest, and</u> started catching them. The man bought thousands at $10, (64)<u>and,</u> as the supply started to diminish, the villagers let (65)<u>there</u> efforts lag. The man (66)<u>later</u> announced that he would buy monkeys at $20 each. This renewed the vigor of the (67)<u>villagers and</u> got them catching monkeys again.

Soon the supply diminished even further, and people started going back to their farms. The offer was increased, this time to $25 each, and the supply of monkeys became so (68)<u>few</u> that it was an effort (69)<u>to even see</u> a monkey, (70)<u>let alone catch one</u>!

Well, the man now decided to raise his price (71)<u>again he announced</u> that he would buy monkeys at $50! However, since he had to go to the city on some business, he introduced the villagers to his assistant. "My assistant's name is Eddie. Here he is. (72)<u>This is him</u>. While I am away, Eddie will be the one who buys the monkeys, (73)<u>not me</u>."

With the man gone, Eddie (74)<u>tells</u> the villagers, "Look, I have a great idea. Look at all these monkeys in the big cage that the man has collected. I will sell them to you at $35 and when he gets back from the city, you can easily sell them to him for $50 each."

The villagers all thought this was an excellent idea. They collected their savings, rounded up all the money they could find, and proceeded to buy back all of the monkeys. Eddie took their money and disappeared into the forest. The villagers waited for the first man to return from the city, so they could sell him the monkeys for $50, but he never came. They never again saw him or his assistant, Eddie, (75)<u>only monkeys everywhere</u>!

61. A. no change
    B. there was once
    C. in
    D. there is

62. F. no change
    G. Since
    H. Seeing that
    J. Noticing that

63. A. no change
    B. forest and
    C. woods, and
    D. skillfully

64. F. no change
    G. since
    H. when
    J. but

65. A. no change
    B. OMIT this word
    C. they're
    D. their

66. F. no change
    G. OMIT this word
    H. soon
    J. kindly

67. A. no change
    B. villagers though
    C. townspeople, and
    D. villagers, and

68. F. no change
    G. OMIT this word
    H. limited
    J. distracted

69. A. no change
    B. even to see
    C. to see even
    D. to see

70. F. no change
    G. not only catch one
    H. let alone to catch one
    J. if only to catch one

71. A. no change
    B. again; he announced
    C. again, he announced
    D. again…he announced

72. F. no change
    G. This is Eddie.
    H. This is Ed.
    J. This is he.

73. A. no change
    B. not I
    C. despite me
    D. with me

74. F. no change
    G. speaks to
    H. told
    J. went to

75. A. no change
    B. instead of them they saw monkeys
    C. because of the monkeys
    D. so they looked at the monkeys

Mathematics

1. Of the following expressions, which is equal to $6\sqrt{10}$?
    A. 36
    B. $\sqrt{600}$
    C. $\sqrt{360}$
    D. $\sqrt{6}$
    E. $10\sqrt{6}$

2. A box of laundry detergent contains 16.5 oz of product. What is the maximum number of loads that can be washed if each load requires a minimum of ¾ oz of detergent?
    F. 10 loads
    G. 50 loads
    H. 22 loads
    J. 18 loads
    K. 16.5 loads

3. Which of the following graphs could represent the equation $y = -3x + 2$?

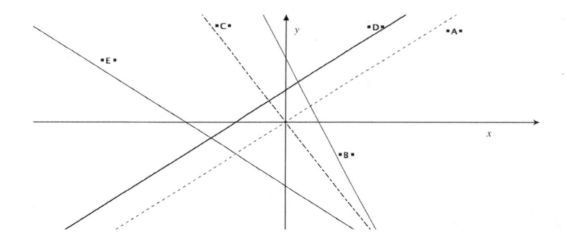

4. There are n musicians in a marching band. All play either a drum or a brass instrument. If p represents the fraction of musicians playing drums, how many play a brass instrument?
    F. $pn - 1$
    G. $p(n-1)$
    H. $(p-1)n$
    J. $(p+1)n$
    K. $(1-p)n$

5. Given the triangle shown in the figure, what is the length of the side A?

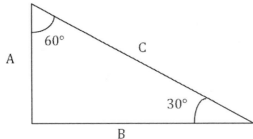

A. C/2
B. B/2
C. (B+C)/2
D. 2B
E. 2C

6. Which of the following can be divided by 3, with no remainder?
   F. 2018
   G. 46
   H. 8912
   J. 555
   K. 739

7. A bullet travels at 5×10^6 feet per hour. If it strikes its target in 2×10^{-4} hours, how far has it traveled?
   A. 50 feet
   B. 25 feet
   C. 100 feet
   D. 1000 feet
   E. 200 feet

8. If the two lines $2x + y = 0$ and $y = 3$ are plotted on a typical xy coordinate grid, at which point will they intersect?
   F. -1.5, 3
   G. 1.5, 3
   H. -1.5, 0
   J. 4, 1
   K. 4.5, 1

9. Which of the following equations describes a line that is parallel to the x-axis?
   A. $y = 3$
   B. $y = 2x$
   C. $(x + y) = 0$
   D. $y = -3x$
   E. None of the above

Questions 10-12 are based on the following diagram of a circle, where O is the center and OA and OC are radii:

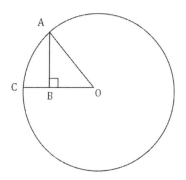

10. If the length of segment AB = x, and the length of segment OB = y, which of the following expressions describes the radius of the circle?

    F. $x + y$

    G. $x^2 + y^2$

    H. $y + 4$

    J. $\sqrt{x^2 + y^2}$

    K. $\sqrt{x^2 + 1}$

11. If the length of segment AB equals that of segment OB, what is the $\angle AOC$?

    A. 45 degrees

    B. Same as $\angle BAO$

    C. Same as $\angle ABO$

    D. All of the above are true

    E. A and B are true, but not C

12. Which of the following must be true?

    F. OA = OC

    G. OB = BC

    H. OB = OC

    J. AB = OC

    K. None of the above

13. A blouse normally sells for $138, but is on sale for 25% off. What is the cost of the blouse?

    A. $67

    B. $103.50

    C. $34.50

    D. $113

    E. $125

14. Which number is equivalent to 2^{-3}?

    F. 1/2

    G. 1/4

    H. 1/8

    J. 1/16

    K. 1/12

15. A straight line with slope +4 is plotted on a standard Cartesian (xy) coordinate system so that it intersects the y-axis at a value of $y = 1$. Which of the following points will the line pass through?

    A. (2, 9)

    B. (0, -1)

    C. (0, 0)

    D. (4, 1)

    E. (1, 4)

16. A crane raises one end of a 3300 lb steel beam. The other end rests upon the ground. If the crane supports 30% of the beam's weight, how many pounds does it support?

    F. 330 lbs

    G. 990 lbs

    H. 700 lbs

    J. 1100 lbs

    K. 2310 lbs

17. $\left|7-5\right|-\left|5-7\right|=?$

    A. 0

    B. 4

    C. 2

    D. -2

    E. -4

18. What is the average of $\dfrac{7}{5}$ and 1.4?

    F. 5.4

    G. 1.4

    H. 2.4

    J. 7.4

    K. None of the above

19. What is the surface area of a cube, in square inches, if the length of one side of the cube is 3 inches?

    A. 9 in^2

    B. 27 in^2

    C. 54 in^2

    D. 18 in^2

    E. 21 in^2

20. Which of the following values is closest to the diameter of a circle with an area of 314 square inches?

   F. 20 inches
   G. 10 inches
   H. 100 inches
   J. 31.4 inches
   K. 2π inches

21. The following table shows the distance from a point to a moving car at various times.

d	Distance	50	70	110
t	Time	2	3	5

If the speed of the car is constant, which of the following equations describes the distance from the point to the car?

   A. $d = 25t$
   B. $d = 35t$
   C. $d = 55t$
   D. $d = 20t + 10$
   E. None of the above

22. A circle has a perimeter of 35 feet. What is its diameter?

   F. 11.14 feet
   G. 6.28 feet
   H. 5.57 feet
   J. 3.5 feet
   K. 14 feet

23. Two angles of a triangle measure 15 and 70 degrees, respectively. What is the size of the third angle?

   A. 90 degrees
   B. 80 degrees
   C. 75 degrees
   D. 125 degrees
   E. 95 degrees

24. The triangle shown in the figure has angles A, B, and C, and sides a, b, and c. If $a = 14$ cm and $b = 12$ cm, and if angle $\angle B = 35$ degrees, what is angle $\angle A$?

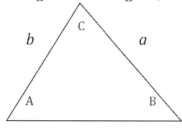

   F. 35 degrees
   G. 42 degrees
   H. 64 degrees
   J. 18 degrees
   K. 28 degrees

- 18 -

25. A metal rod used in manufacturing must be as close as possible to 15 inches in length. The tolerance of the length, L, in inches, is specified by the inequality $| L - 15 | \leq 0.01$. What is the minimum length permissible for the rod?
   A. 14.9 inches
   B. 14.99 inches
   C. 15.01 inches
   D. 15.1 inches
   E. 14.991 inches

26. Two numbers are said to be reciprocal if their product equals 1. Which of the following represents the reciprocal of the variable x?
   F. $x-1$
   G. $\dfrac{1}{x}$
   H. x^{-1}
   J. x^{-2}
   K. Both G and H

27. A taxi service charges $5.50 for the first 1/5 of a mile, $1.50 for each additional 1/5 of a mile, and 20¢ per minute of waiting time. Joan took a cab from her home to a flower shop 8 miles away, where she bought a bouquet, and then another 3.6 miles to her mother's house. The driver had to wait 9 minutes while she bought the bouquet. What was the fare?
   A. $20
   B. $120.20
   C. $92.80
   D. $91
   E. $90

28. Which of the following expressions is equivalent to the equation $3x^2 + 4x - 15$?
   F. $(x-3)(x+5)$
   G. $(x+5)(3+x^2)$
   H. $x(3x+4-15)$
   J. $(3x^2+5)(x-5)$
   K. $(x+3)(3x-5)$

29. Prizes are to be awarded to the best pupils in each class of an elementary school. The number of students in each grade is shown in the table, and the school principal wants the number of prizes awarded in each grade to be proportional to the number of students. If there are twenty prizes, how many should go to fifth-grade students?

Grade	1	2	3	4	5
Students	35	38	38	33	36

   A. 5
   B. 4
   C. 7
   D. 3
   E. 2

30. An MP3 player is set to play songs at random from the fifteen songs it contains in its memory. Any song can be played at any time, even if it is repeated. There are 5 songs by Band A, 3 songs by Band B, 2 by Band C, and 5 by Band D. If the player has just played two songs in a row by Band D, what is the probability that the next song will also be by Band D?

    F. 1 in 5
    G. 1 in 3
    H. 1 in 9
    J. 1 in 27
    K. Not enough data to determine

31. Referring again to the MP3 player described in Question 30, what is the probability that the next two songs will both be by Band B?

    A. 1 in 25
    B. 1 in 3
    C. 1 in 5
    D. 1 in 9
    E. Not enough data to determine

32. Which of the following numbers is a prime number?

    F. 15
    G. 11
    H. 33
    J. 4
    K. 88

33. Which of the following expressions is equivalent to $3(\dfrac{6x-3}{3})-3(9x+9)$?

    A. $-3(7x+10)$
    B. $-3x+6$
    C. $(x+3)(x-3)$
    D. $3x^2-9$
    E. $15x-9$

34. Evaluate the expression $(x-2y)^2$, where x = 3 and y = 2.

    F. -1
    G. +1
    H. +4
    J. -2
    K. -3

35. For the figure shown, if the length of segment AB is twice the length of segment AD, what is the relationship between segments AC and EC?

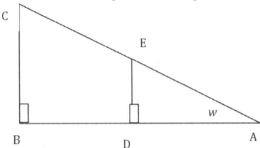

A. AC = 2EC

B. AC = $\sqrt{2}$ EC

C. EC = $\sqrt{2}$ AC

D. EC = 2AC

E. Cannot be determined

36. A circle is inscribed within a square, as shown. What is the difference between the area of the square and that of the circle, where r is the radius of the circle?

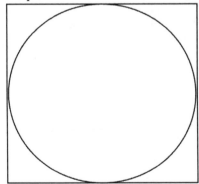

F. 2π

G. $\frac{4}{3}\pi r^3$

H. $r^2(4 - \pi)$

J. $2\pi r$

K. $2r^2$

37. Two circles of identical size are adjacent, but non-overlapping, and are inscribed within a rectangle as shown. If the area of the rectangle is 32 square meters, what is the area of one of the circles?

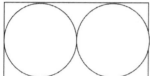

A. 8 m^2

B. 16 m^2

C. 2π m^2

D. 4π m^2

E. Cannot be determined

38. An investigator, working for a sporting league, suspects that a ball that is used for one of the contests may have been filled with cork in order to alter the way it responds when hit. To test his suspicion, he weighs the ball. The density of cork is 3 gm/cm³, whereas the normal filling has a density of 4 gm/cm³. The diameter of the ball is 6 cm. If the ball has not been tampered with, how much should it weigh?

F. 16.75 gm

G. 602.88 gm

H. 150.8 gm

J. 211.45 gm

K. 452.16 gm

39. Please refer to the description in question 38. The investigator weighs the ball, and finds that it weighs 413.38 gm. Assuming that the cork filler is also spherical, what is the radius of the cork plug?

A. 2.10 cm

B. 3.10 cm

C. 3.25 cm

D. 4.11 cm

E. 1.14 cm

40. Bob decides to go into business selling lemonade. He buys a wooden stand for $45, and sets it up outside of his house. He figures that the cost of lemons, sugar, and paper cups for each glass of lemonade sold will be 10¢. Which of these expressions describes his cost for making g glasses of lemonade?

F. $45 + $0.1 x g

G. $44.90 x g

H. $44.90 x g + 10¢

J. $90

K. $45.10

41. Which of the following expressions is equivalent to $(3x^{-2})^3$?

A. $9x^{-6}$

B. $9x^{-8}$

C. $27x^{-8}$

D. $27x^{-4}$

E. $27x^{-6}$

42. Sally wants to buy a used truck for her delivery business. Truck A is priced at $450 and gets 25 miles per gallon. Truck B costs $650 and gets 35 miles per gallon. If gasoline costs $4 per gallon, how many miles must Sally drive to make truck B the better buy?

F. 600 miles

G. 7500 miles

H. 340 miles

J. 4375 miles

K. 1600 miles

43. To determine a student's grade, a teacher throws out the lowest grade obtained on 5 tests, averages the remaining grades, and then rounds the grade up to the nearest integer. If Betty scored 72, 75, 88, 86, and 90 on her tests, what grade will she receive?

A. 68

B. 85

C. 88

D. 84.8

E. 84

44. There is a big sale taking place at the clothing store on Main Street. Everything is marked down by 33% from the original price, p. Which of the following expressions describes the sale price, S, to be paid for any item?

F. $S = p - 0.33$

G. $S = p - 0.33p$

H. $S = 0.33p$

J. $S = 0.33(1-p)$

K. $S = p + 0.33p$

45. The town of Fram will build a water storage tank on a hill overlooking the town. The tank will be a right, circular cylinder of radius R, and height H. The plot of ground selected for the installation is large enough to accommodate a circular tank 60 feet in diameter. The planning commission wants the tank to hold 1,000,000 cubic feet of water, and they intend to use the full area available. Which of the following is the minimum acceptable height?

A. 655 ft

B. 455 ft

C. 354 ft

D. 255 ft

E. 155 ft

46. A package is dropped from an airplane. The height of the package at any time, t, is described by the equation: $y(t) = -\frac{1}{2}at^2 + v_o + h_o$,

where y is the height, h_o is the original height, or the altitude from which it was dropped, a is the acceleration due to gravity, v_o is the original velocity, and t is the time. The value of a is 32 ft/sec². If the airplane is flying at 30,000 feet, what is the altitude of the package 15 seconds after it is dropped?

F. 29,520 ft

- 23 -

G. 26,400 ft
H. 22,800 ft
J. 7,200 ft
K. 0 ft

47. Five numbered-equations are plotted on an *xy* coordinate system in the figure below.

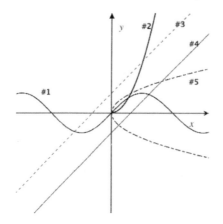

One of these curves corresponds to the equation $y = \sin(x)$. Which one is it?
    A. Curve #1
    B. Curve #2
    C. Curve #3
    D. Curve #4
    E. Curve #5

48. Refer again to the figure in Question 47. One of the curves corresponds to the equation $x = y - 1$. Which one is it?
    F. Curve #1
    G. Curve #2
    H. Curve #3
    J. Curve #4
    K. Curve #5

49. Refer again to the figure in Question 47. One of the curves corresponds to the equation $x = \sqrt{y}$.. Which one is it?
    A. Curve #1
    B. Curve #2
    C. Curve #3
    D. Curve #4
    E. Curve #5

50. Refer again to the figure in Question 47. One of the curves corresponds to the equation $x = y + 1$. Which one is it?
    F. Curve #1
    G. Curve #2
    H. Curve #3
    J. Curve #4
    K. Curve #5

51. Refer again to the figure in Question 47. One of the curves corresponds to the equation $x = y^2$. Which one is it?

    A. Curve #1
    B. Curve #2
    C. Curve #3
    D. Curve #4
    E. Curve #5

52. A rock group with 5 musicians gets 25% of the gross sales of their new album, but they have to give their agent 15% of their share. If the album grosses $20,000,000, what is each band member's share?

    F. $850,000
    G. $4,000,000
    H. $1,150,000
    J. $650,000
    K. $800,000

53. Given the equation $\dfrac{3}{y-5} = \dfrac{15}{y+4}$, what is the value of y?

    A. 45
    B. 54
    C. $\dfrac{29}{4}$
    D. $\dfrac{4}{29}$
    E. $\dfrac{4}{45}$

54. Given the equations for two straight lines,
$ax + 3y = 18$ and
$15x + ay = 24$,
what positive value of the constant a would make the lines parallel in the standard xy coordinate plane?

    F. 6
    G. $\sqrt{45}$
    H. $\sqrt{18}$
    J. 45^2
    K. 6^2

55. At a school with *n* students, Friday is declared Hat Day. If *p*% of the students show up wearing hats, which of the following expressions describes the number of students not wearing hats?

A. $1 - p$

B. $0.01np$

C. $\dfrac{(100 - p)}{100} \times n$

D. $\dfrac{(100 - pn)}{100}$

E. $1 - pn$

56. In a particle accelerator, a neutrino travels in a straight line at a velocity of 1×10^6 meters per second. If it travels for 3×10^{-11} seconds, what is the distance traveled?

F. 0.3×10^{-5} meters

G. 3×10^{-5} meters

H. 0.3×10^5 meters

J. 3×10^5 meters

K. 0.33×10^5 meters

57. The weight in pounds of five students is 112, 112, 116, 133, and 145. What is the median weight of the group?

A. 123.6 lbs

B. 116 lbs

C. 112 lbs

D. 118.5 lbs

E. 140 lbs

58. Which of the following expressions is equivalent to $(a)(a)(a)(a)(a)$ for all values of *a*, positive or negative?

F. $5a$

G. a^{-5}

H. $a^{-\frac{1}{5}}$

J. a^5

K. $5a^{\frac{1}{5}}$

59. Which value is equivalent to 7.5×10^{-4}?

A. 0.075

B. 0.00075

C. 0.0075

D. 0.75

E. 0.0030

60. How many real-number solutions exist for the equation $x^2 + 1 = 0$?

    F. 0

    G. 1

    H. 2

    J. 3

    K. 4

Reading

Questions 1-10 pertain to the following passage:

    This Passage Is A Re-Telling Of A Traditional American Indian Legend.

<u>The Black Crow.</u>

In ancient times, the people hunted the buffalo on the Great Plains. These huge animals were their source of food and clothing. With stone-tipped spears, they stalked the great beasts through the tall grasses. It was difficult and dangerous work, but they were forced to do it in order to survive.

At that time, there were many crows flying above the plains, as there are today. But unlike the crows we see now, these birds were white. And they were friends to the buffalo, which caused the hunters no end of travail. The white crows flew high above the plains, where they could see all that was happening below. And when they saw that hunters were approaching the herd, they would warn the buffalo. Swooping down low, they would land on the heads of the great beasts and call out to them: "Beware! Beware! Hunters are coming from the south! Caw, caw. Beware!" And the buffalo would stampede, leaving the hunters empty-handed.

This went on for some time, until the people were hungry, and something needed to be done. A council was convened, and the chief of the people spoke to them. "We must capture the chief of the crows, and teach him a lesson, he said. If we can frighten him, he will stop warning the buffalo when our hunters approach, and the other crows will stop as well."

The old chief then brought out a buffalo skin, one with the head and horns still attached. "With this, we can capture the chief of the crows," he said. And he gave the skin to one of the tribe's young braves, a man known as Long Arrow. "Disguise yourself with this, and hide among the buffalo in the herd," the chief told Long Arrow. "Then, when the chief of the crows approaches, you will capture him and bring him back to the tribe."

So Long Arrow donned the buffalo skin disguise and went out onto the plains. Carefully, he approached a large herd of buffalo and mingled among them, pretending to graze upon the grasses. He moved slowly with the herd as they sought fresh food, and he waited for the great white bird that was the chief of the crows.

The other braves made ready for the hunt. They prepared their stone-tipped spears and arrows, and they approached the grazing herd of beasts, hiding in ravines and

- 27 -

behind rocks to try to sneak up on them. But the crows, flying high in the sky, saw everything. The chief of the crows saw the men in the ravines and tall grasses, and eventually he came gliding down to warn the buffalo of the approaching hunters.

Hearing the great white crow's warning, the herd ran from the hunters. All stampeded across the plains except Long Arrow, still in his disguise. Seeing that Long Arrow remained, and thinking that he was a buffalo like all the others, the great white crow flew to him and landed upon his head. "Caw, caw. Hunters are approaching! Have you not heard my warning? Why do you remain here?" But as the great bird cried out, Long Arrow reached from under his disguise and grabbed the bird's feet, capturing him. He pushed him into a rawhide bag and brought him back to the tribal council.

The people debated what to do with the chief of the crows. Some wanted to cut his wings, so that he could not fly. Some wanted to kill him, and some wanted to remove his feathers as punishment for making the tribe go hungry. Finally, one brave strode forward in anger, grabbed the rawhide bag that held the bird, and before anyone could prevent it, threw it into the fire.

As the fire burned the rawhide bag, the big bird struggled to escape. Finally, he succeeded in getting out of the bag and managed to fly out of the fire, but his feathers were singed and covered with black soot from the fire. The chief of the crows was no longer white; he was black – as crows are today.

And from that day forward, all crows have been black. And although they fly above the plains and can see all that transpires below, they no longer warn the buffalo that hunters are approaching.

1. According to the passage, the people used stone spears to hunt the buffalo because
    A. They had no metal.
    B. They had no horses.
    C. They needed to eat.
    D. They were plentiful.

2. The word *travail* (Line 9) means
    F. Travel.
    G. Difficulty.
    H. Anger.
    J. Fear.

3. Which statement best describes what the chief of the crows represents in this passage?
    A. He symbolizes all that is evil.
    B. He is a symbol representing all crows.
    C. He represents the animal kingdom.
    D. He represents other predators who compete with the tribe.

4. Which of the following best describes the people's motivation for wanting to capture the chief of the crows?
    F. They hated birds.
    G. They wanted to turn him black.
    H. They wanted to eat him.
    J. They were hungry.

5. Long Arrow's activities among the herd while disguised imply that he
    A. Had time to kill.
    B. Wanted to fool the buffalo.
    C. Wanted to fool the crows.
    D. Had forgotten his stone-tipped spear.

6. In this tale, the rawhide bag and stone-tipped spears are both details that
    F. Are important for the outcome of the tale.
    G. Paint a picture of the primitive culture of the people.
    H. Make it clear that the people were dependent upon the buffalo.
    J. Show how the people hunted.

7. Why might the chief of the crows have landed upon Long Arrow's head after seeing the other buffalo stampede away?
    A. He thought his warning had not been heard.
    B. He wanted to see the disguise.
    C. He thought that Long Arrow was an injured buffalo.
    D. He had no fear of men.

8. Once the bird has been caught, what emotions are revealed by the people's deliberations about how to deal with him?
    F. Anger
    G. A calm resolve to change the birds' behavior
    H. A feeling of celebration now that the bird has been caught
    J. Hunger

9. What does the story tell us about why Long Arrow was selected for this task?
    A. He was the bravest man in the tribe.
    B. He was related to the chief.
    C. He was able to act like a buffalo.
    D. The story says nothing about why he was selected.

10. What does this story suggest that the American Indians thought of crows?
    F. They were dirty animals.
    G. They were clever animals.
    H. They were selfish animals.
    J. They disliked the people in the tribe.

Questions 11-20 pertain to the following passage:
This passage is adapted from "Sailing Around the World" by Capt. Joshua Slocum (1899).
I had not been in Buenos Aires for a number of years. The place where I had once landed from packets in a cart was now built up with magnificent docks. Vast

fortunes had been spent in remodeling the harbor; London bankers could tell you that. The port captain after assigning the *Spray* a safe berth with his compliments sent me word to call on him for anything I might want while in port and I felt quite sure that his friendship was sincere. The sloop was well cared for at Buenos Aires; her dockage and tonnage dues were all free, and the yachting fraternity of the city welcomed her with a good will. In town, I found things not so greatly changed as about the docks and I soon felt myself more at home.

From Montevideo I had forwarded a letter from Sir Edward Hairby to the owner of the "Standard", MrMulhall, and in reply to it was assured of a warm welcome to the warmest heart, I think, outside of Ireland. MrMulhall, with a prancing team, came down to the docks as soon as the Spray was berthed, and would have me go to his house at once, where a room was waiting. And it was New Year's day, 1896. The course of the *Spray* had been followed in the columns of the "Standard."

MrMulhall kindly drove me to see many improvements about the city, and we went in search of some of the old landmarks. The man who sold lemonade on the plaza when first I visited this wonderful city I found selling lemonade still at two cents a glass; he had made a fortune by it. His stock in trade was a wash tub and a neighboring hydrant, a moderate supply of brown sugar, and about six lemons that floated on the sweetened water. The water from time to time was renewed from the friendly pump. but the lemon "went on forever," and all at two cents a glass.

But we looked in vain for the man who once sold whisky and coffins in Buenos Aires; the march of civilization had crushed him -- memory only clung to his name. Enterprising man that he was, I fain would have looked him up. I remember the tiers of whisky barrels, ranged on end, on one side of the store, while on the other side, and divided by a thin partition, were the coffins in the same order, of all sizes and in great numbers. The unique arrangement seemed in order, for as a cask was emptied a coffin might be filled. Besides cheap whisky and many other liquors, he sold "cider" which he manufactured from damaged Malaga raisins. Within the scope of his enterprise was also the sale of mineral waters, not entirely blameless of the germs of disease. This man surely catered to all the tastes, wants, and conditions of his customers.

Farther along in the city, however, survived the good man who wrote on the side of his store, where thoughtful men might read and learn: "This wicked world will be destroyed by a comet! The owner of this store is therefore bound to sell out at any price and avoid the catastrophe." My friend MrMulhall drove me round to view the fearful comet with streaming tail pictured large on the merchant's walls.

11. The passage suggests that the *Spray* was
    A. A packet.
    B. A sailboat.
    C. A bus.
    D. A jet of water.

12. The author found that, since his previous visit, the greatest changes in Buenos Aires had taken place:
    F. Downtown.
    G. At the harbor.
    H. At a lemonade stand.
    J. At the bank.

13. The author was shown around Buenos Aires by Mr. Mulhall. How did he come to know Mr. Mulhall?
    A. They had previously met in Ireland.
    B. They had met on the author's first visit to the city.
    C. They met through a letter of introduction.
    D. They met on the docks.

14. The passage suggests that the "Standard" was
    F. A steam packet.
    G. A sailboat.
    H. A newspaper.
    J. An ocean chart.

15. The author uses the term "landmarks" to refer to
    A. Monuments.
    B. Merchants.
    C. Banks.
    D. Buildings.

16. The passage suggests that the lemonade vendor used fresh lemons
    F. Whenever the flavor got weak.
    G. Every morning.
    H. Almost never.
    J. When he could get them.

17. The meaning of the word "fain" (Line 27) is closest to
    A. Anxiously.
    B. Willingly.
    C. Desperately.
    D. Indifferently.

18. The description of the mineral waters sold by the whiskey merchant (line 32) suggests that these waters
    F. Could cure disease.
    G. Were held in casks.
    H. Were not very clean.
    J. Were mixed with the cider.

19. The passage suggests that the merchant with the picture of the comet on his walls had
    A. Malaga raisins.
    B. Been in Buenos Aires when the author first visited.
    C. Painted the sign himself.
    D. Lived for a very long time.

20. The sign warning that a comet would cause the end of the world was most likely
    F. An advertising gimmick.
    G. A reflection of the merchant's paranoia.
    H. A way to cover an unsightly wall.
    J. Written about in the "Standard."

Questions 21-30 pertain to the following passage:

Ernst Lubitsch

The comedy of manners was a style of film popular in the 1930s. These movies expressed the frustrations of the depression-era poor by mocking the swells of the upper classes, and contrasting their gilded lives to the daily grind of the downtrodden masses. One of the greatest directors of this type of film was Ernst Lubitsch, a German filmmaker who eventually came to Hollywood to make some of his greatest films.

Lubitsch's film career began in the silent era. Born in Berlin, in 1982, he worked at first as an actor, subsequently debuting as a director with the film *Passion* in 1912. He made more than 40 films in Germany, but the advent of sound brought him to Hollywood, where the new technology was most readily available. After the producer Albert Zukor invited him to come to the U.S. in 1923, he pursued his career in the capital of film until the late 1940s. His signature style – a focus on seemingly insignificant details that imbued them with symbolism in the context of the film – was just as effective in the "talkies" as it had been in silent films. One of his greatest comedies, *Trouble in Paradise*, starred Herbert Marshall and Miriam Hopkins and was shot in 1932. A stinging social comedy that skewers the illusions of the upper classes, it would not have been well received in his native Germany of the time.

Trouble in Paradise tells the story of a charming, elegant thief. Marshall plays Gaston Monescu, a man whose charm and elegant manners allow him to work his way into the bosom of high society. In the hotels and clubs of the rich, he manages to gain the trust of wealthy individuals until he swindles them. Monescu courts the rich perfume heiress, Mariette, and we are never certain of how sincere his affection for her may be. But he is also in love with his accomplice, Lily, a clever thief in her own right. His eventual decision to leave Mariette for her can be seen as an affirmation of the unity of the working class in this very class-conscious film.

The opening scenes of the film provide a classic example of Lubitsch's wry symbolism. The opening shot is of a garbage can, which is duly picked up by a garbage man and dumped onto what seems to be a truck. But, as the camera pans back, we realize that the truck is, in fact, a gondola, and that the scene takes place in Venice. As the gondolier-garbage man breaks into a romantic song, the camera contrasts the elegant city, it's palaces and beautiful canals, with the mundane reality of garbage and necessary, low-wage work.

The film continues to contrast the elegant surfaces of society with the corruption that lies beneath. A classic scene is the first meeting between Monescu and Lily, two thieves with polished manners. In an elegant hotel room, the two engage in a genteel banter filled with seductive double-entendres and urbane banalities. But they are not the Baron and Countess they profess to be, as their behavior soon makes clear. As the supper progresses, they manage to steal one another's wallets, jewelry, and watches. Finally, they reveal the thefts to one another and sort out their belongings, but Monescu has been won over by Lily's cleverness, for he admires her resourcefulness far more than the undeserved wealth of the upper classes.

Lubitsch went on to make many more films during the 1930s, comedies of manners and musical comedies as well. Among his greatest Hollywood films are *Design for Living* (1933), *The Merry Widow* (1934), *Ninotchka* (1939), and *Heaven Can Wait* (1943). One of the wittiest directors of all time, he made films in English, German and French, always exhibiting the sharpest eye for detail. His films challenged the intellect of his viewers, and they never disappointed. The juxtaposition of seemingly contradictory elements was always central to his style, as he exposed the falsehoods he found in his world.

21. Which of the following terms would not be a good description of Lubitsch's film style, as it is described in the text?
    A. Sophisticated
    B. Erudite
    C. Chic
    D. Boisterous

22. One of the tools that Lubitsch used to mock the upper classes, as shown in the text, was
    F. Lighting.
    G. Talking pictures.
    H. Juxtaposition of contradictory elements.
    J. Urbane banalities.

23. Lubitsch's signature style can be described as
    A. Double-entendres and urbane banalities.
    B. Using apparently insignificant details as symbols.
    C. Charm and elegant manners.
    D. Corruption underlying high society.

24. Lubitsch first came to the U.S in 1923 because
    F. His films were not well received in Germany.
    G. He was fleeing the Nazi regime.
    H. He was invited by a producer.
    J. He could not make films with sound in Germany.

25. The text tells us that Lubitsch's first film, *Passion* was
    A. An early "talkie."
    B. A comedy of manners.
    C. A film starring Miriam Hopkins.
    D. None of the above.

26. Without considering gender, which two characters have the most in common?
    F. Monescu and Lily
    G. Monescu and Mariette
    H. Lily and Mariette
    J. Monescu and Lubitsch

27. The scene with the garbage gondola at the opening of the film shows that
    A. The rich need supporting services.
    B. Venice is kept clean by gondoliers.
    C. Elegance may be only a veneer.
    D. Gondoliers sing romantic ballads.

28. Monescu most admires
    F. Lily's wealth.
    G. Lily's cleverness.
    H. Mariette's money.
    J. Venetian gondolas.

29. In the film, Lily pretends to be
    A. A perfume heiress.
    B. A countess.
    C. A wealthy dowager.
    D. Monescu's partner.

30. In addition to the films he made in Hollywood and Germany, the text suggests that
Lubitsch made movies in
    F. England.
    G. France.
    H. Spain.
    J. Lisbon.

Questions 31-40 pertain to the following passage:

Cilia and Flagella

Cilia and flagella are tubular structures found on the surfaces of many animal cells. They are examples of organelles, sub-cellular structures that perform a particular function. By beating against the surrounding medium in a swimming motion, they may endow cells with motility or induce the medium to circulate, as in the case of gills. Ciliated cells typically each contain large numbers of cilia 2 -10 μm (micrometer) long. In contrast, flagellated cells usually have one or two flagella, and the structures can be as long as 200 μm. For both types of structure, the diameters are less than 0.5 μm.

Although they share similar structures, the motion of the two organelles is somewhat different. Flagella beat in a circular, undulating motion that is continuous. The effective stroke of a cilium's beat, which generates the power, is followed by a more languid recovery to the original position. During the recovery stroke, they are brought in close to the membrane of the cell. Cilia usually beat in coordinated waves, so that at any given moment some are in the midst of their power stroke while

- 34 -

others are recovering. This provides for a steady flow of fluid past gill surfaces or the epithelia lining the lungs or digestive tract.

The construction of both organelles is very similar. A portion of the cell membrane appears to be stretched over a framework made of tubulin polymers. A polymer is a long, chain-like molecule made of smaller units that are strung together. In this case, the subunits are molecules of the protein tubulin. The framework, or skeleton, of a cilium or flagellum consists of 9 pairs of tubulin polymers spaced around the periphery, and two more single polymers of tubulin that run along the center of the shaft. This is called a 9+2 pattern.

The motion of the organelles results from chemical reactions that cause the outer polymers to slide past one another. By doing so, they force the overall structure to bend. This is similar to the mechanism of contraction of skeletal muscle. In cilia and flagella, the nine outer polymer pairs of the skeleton have along their lengths molecules of a rod-shaped protein called dynein. The dynein rods can grasp, or bind to, the neighboring tubulin polymer. Energy is then used to drive a chemical reaction that causes the dynein arms to bend, causing one tubulin polymer to move along the length of the other. Through a coordinated series of thousands of such reactions, the cilium or flagellum will beat.

Cilia have also provided some of the best evidence for the inheritance of traits by a mechanism that does not involve DNA. *Paramecium* is a single-celled ciliated protist that lives in ponds. In one variety, the stroke cycle of the cilia is clockwise (right-handed). In another variety, it is counter-clockwise (left-handed). When the cells divide, left-handed cells give rise to more left-handed cells, and *vice versa*. T.M. Sonneborn of IndianaUniversity managed to cut tiny pieces of cell membrane from a left-handed *Paramecium* and graft them onto a right-handed one. The cell survived, and the direction of the stroke did not change, despite the fact that cilia were now in a cell with a right-handed nucleus and surrounded by right-handed cilia, they continued to rotate to the left. A *paramecium* reproduces by dividing, and Sonneborn followed the transplanted patch for several generations, but it did not change direction. This suggested that the direction of rotation is a property of the cilium itself, and is not influenced by the DNA in the nucleus. In another experiment, Sonneborn transplanted the nucleus of a right-handed cell into a left-handed cell from which the original nucleus had been removed. The cell's cilia kept their counter-clockwise direction of rotation. Further, when this cell divided, all subsequent generations maintained it as well. This proved that the direction of rotation could be inherited in a manner completely independent of the chromosomal DNA.

One theory to explain this is the concept of *nucleation*. According to this idea, the tubulin proteins in left- and right-handed *Paramecia* are the same, so that the genes that give rise to them are also identical. However, once they begin to chain together in a left- or right-handed manner, they continue to do so. Therefore the direction of rotation does not depend upon the genes, but rather on some basal structure that is passed on to the cell's offspring when it divides.

31. Cilia and flagella are both
    A. Proteins.
    B. Sub-cellular structures that perform a particular function.
    C. Organelles that beat in a continuous undulating motion.
    D. Single-celled protists

32. According to the passage, where would you expect to find cilia?
    F. Stomach lining
    G. Back of the hand
    H. Lining of the heart
    J. Circulatory system

33. According to the passage, how many tubulin polymers make up the entire 9+2 pattern seen in cilia and flagella?
    A. 11
    B. 9
    C. 20
    D. Passage doesn't say

34. Two proteins mentioned in this passage are
    F. Tubulin and Paramecium.
    G. Tubulin and dynein.
    H. Tubulin and flagellin.
    J. Tubulin and Sonneborn.

35. Which of the following describes how the beating motion of flagella is caused?
    A. The two central polymers slide past one another.
    B. Dynein causes the outer polymer pairs to slide past one another.
    C. Dynein causes each of the outer polymers to bend.
    D. The organelle increases in diameter.

36. Polymers are always
    F. Made of protein.
    G. Made of tubulin.
    H. Made of subunits.
    J. Arranged in a 9+2 array.

37. The passage implies that T.M. Sonneborn was
    A. A zookeeper.
    B. A scientist at Indiana University.
    C. A chemist.
    D. A medical practitioner.

38. It was shown that, if cilia with a counterclockwise rotation are grafted onto a cell whose native cilia beat clockwise, the transplants will
    F. Beat clockwise.
    G. Stop beating.
    H. Beat randomly.
    J. Beat counterclockwise.

39. The passage describes cilia and flagella and tells us that
    A. Cilia may be 200 μm long.
    B. Flagella are less than 0.5 μm long.
    C. Cells can have more than two flagella.
    D. Flagella are less than 0.5 μm in diameter.

40. Sonneborn's experiments showed that
    F. Chromosomes influence the inheritance of rotational direction in cilia.
    G. Rotational direction in cilia is inherited by a mechanism that does not involve DNA.
    H. Chromosomes do not influence the inheritance of rotational direction in flagella.
    J. Rotational direction in cilia is random.

Science

Questions 1-8 pertain to the following information:

Blood consists of a liquid called *plasma*, in which many different types of blood cells are suspended. The plasma also contains many dissolved proteins. These proteins may be studied by subjecting the plasma to *electrophoresis*, in which it is subjected to an electric field, which pulls the proteins through a porous gel. Proteins typically have a negative charge on their surface, so they move toward the anode (positive electrode) in an electric field. The gel acts as a molecular sieve: it interferes with the movement, or *migration*, of the larger proteins more than the small ones, allowing the proteins to be separated on the basis of size. The further the proteins move during the experiment, the smaller they must be.

The experiment results in an *electropherogram*, such as the one shown in the figure below. This is a plot, or graph, of protein concentration versus migration, and corresponds to a graph of concentration versus size. Concentration is measured by passing light of a certain wavelength through the gel: proteins absorb the light, and the resulting *absorbance* measurement is proportional to protein concentration. Many major blood component proteins, such as albumin and several identified by Greek letters, have been discovered in this way. When disease is present, some component proteins may break down into smaller fragments. Others may aggregate, or clump together, to form larger fragments. This results in a change in the electropherogram: new species, corresponding to the aggregates or breakdown products, may be present, and the sizes of the normal peaks may be changed as the concentration of normal products is altered.

The Figure shows an electropherogram from a sick patient with an abnormal component in her blood (arrow). Peaks corresponding to some normal plasma proteins have been labeled. Please examine the electropherogram and answer the following questions.

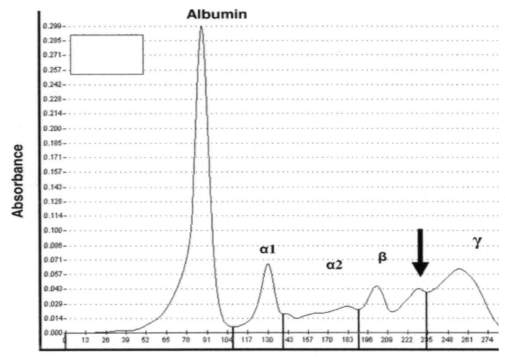

1. Which blood component protein is present in the greatest amounts in the plasma?
   A. Albumin
   B. $\alpha 1$
   C. $\alpha 2$
   D. β

2. Which of the following is the fastest-moving component in the electropherogram?
   F. Albumin
   G. $\alpha 1$
   H. $\alpha 2$
   J. γ

3. Which of the following statements is true about component $\alpha 1$?
   A. The molecules move through the gel faster than those of component $\alpha 2$, but slower than Albumin.
   B. The molecules are larger than albumin, but smaller than all the other components.
   C. The molecules are smaller than albumin, but larger than all the other components.
   D. It is not a protein.

4. Which of the components identified on the electropherogram is the smallest molecule?
   F. Albumin
   G. $\alpha 1$
   H. $\alpha 2$
   J. γ

5. Which of the following is true of the unknown component identified by the arrow?

    A. The molecules are larger than the β component, but smaller than albumin

    B. The molecules are larger than the β component, but smaller than the γ component.

    C. The molecules move more slowly in the gel than all the other components except one.

    D. The molecules move more rapidly in the gel than all the other components except one.

6. Which of the following may be true of the unknown component identified by the arrow?

    F. It is formed of albumin molecules that have aggregated.

    G. It is formed of $\alpha 1$ molecules that have aggregated.

    H. It is formed of $\alpha 2$ molecules that have aggregated.

    J. It is formed of γ molecules that have aggregated.

7. Which of the following may not be true of the unknown component identified by the arrow?

    A. It is formed of albumin molecules that have broken down into fragments.

    B. It is formed of $\alpha 1$ molecules that have broken down into fragments.

    C. It is formed of $\alpha 2$ molecules that have broken down into fragments.

    D. It is formed of γ molecules that have broken down into fragments.

8. The blood of healthy individuals does not contain the unknown component indicated by the arrow. The experiment therefore proves

    F. The unknown component causes the patient's sickness.

    G. The unknown component results from the patient's sickness.

    H. The more of the unknown component there is, the sicker the patient will be.

    J. None of the above.

Questions 9-16 pertain to the following information:

    In a study performed to determine the migration patterns of fish, 34,000 juvenile sablefish of the species *Anoplopoma fimbria* were tagged and released into waters of the eastern Gulf of Alaska during a twenty-year period. The tagged fish were all juveniles (less than 2 years of age), so that the age of the recovered fish could be determined from the date on the tag. This allowed age-specific movement patterns to be studied. Tagged fish were recovered from sites in the Bering Sea, throughout the Gulf of Alaska, and off the coast of British Columbia. The fish were recovered by commercial fishermen, with the results reported to the scientists performing the study. A total of 2011 tagged fish were recovered. It was found that fish spawned in coastal waters move to deeper waters when they are older. At the same time, they migrate north and west, across the Gulf of Alaska toward the Aleutian Islands. Eventually, they return to the eastern Gulf as adults.

    The figure shows tag recoveries from sablefish tagged as juveniles by age (in years) and by depth (in meters) for all the areas in the study. The size of each circle is proportional to the number of recoveries. The range for each data point is 1 to 57 recoveries. The symbol x represents the median age.

Recovery age (yr)

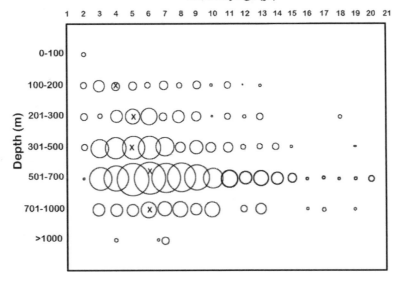

9. If a circle in the graph is twice the size (area) of another circle, this indicates that:
    A. It represents twice as many fish.
    B. The fish it represents were twice as old.
    C. Both A and B.
    D. None of the above.

10. The greatest number of tagged fish were recovered at depths of
    F. 101 – 200 m.
    G. 201 – 300 m.
    H. 301 – 500 m.
    J. 501 – 700 m.

11. What percentage of the released, tagged fish were recovered for this study?
    A. 2011
    B. 20
    C. 6
    D. Can't determine from the data given.

12. The median age of tagged fish recovered at depths between 301 and 500 meters is approximately
    F. 2 years.
    G. 5 years.
    H. 9 years.
    J. Data not shown.

13. Not all the tagged fish were recovered in this study. Which of the following reasons may be responsible for the losses?
    A. Some fish died during the study.
    B. The tags fell off some of the fish during the study.
    C. Some fish die as a result of being tagged.
    D. All of the above.

14. The largest fish are found at depths of
    F. 101 – 200 m.
    G. 201 – 300 m.
    H. 301 – 500 m.
    J. Can't determine from the data given.

15. Which of the following statements is supported by the data in the figure?
    A. Fish return to the eastern Gulf of Alaska to spawn.
    B. Sablefish move progressively deeper with age.
    C. Sablefish prefer cold waters.
    D. Younger fish swim faster than older ones.

16. The data indicate that sablefish may live as long as
    F. 10 years.
    G. 30 years.
    H. 20 years.
    J. 5 years.

Questions 17-24 pertain to the following information:

Most particles studied by physicists are unstable. Given enough time, an unstable particle will break apart into two or more smaller particles or fragments. This event is called a decay. By carefully observing and logically classifying these decays according to some well-understood laws of nature, particle physicists have built a catalog of subatomic particles down to their most fundamental constituent parts.

Some particles, like the proton and electron, appear to be stable for very long times. They don't change into other particles, which is to say they don't decay. Most other particles have dominant decay modes. They decay into one combination of particles more often than into other combinations. Many particles also have rare decay modes. Someone who has the patience to watch a million or so decays, might see one of these rare combinations.

Two of the laws of nature that have been used to understand decays are *conservation of charge* and *conservation of energy*. Conservation of charge says that the net charge of all particles produced in a decay should equal the total charge of the original particle. Conservation of energy implies that the total mass of the resulting particles should not be greater than the mass of the original particle. Mass does not seem to be conserved in many decays until one accounts for the mass that is converted into the kinetic energy of the resulting particles as they move away from the original center of mass at some nonzero speed. Mass and energy can be measured with the same units: particle physicists use MeV (1.000 mega-electron volt = 1.602×10^{-13} joule = 1.783×10^{-30} kilogram).

At the most fundamental level, matter is thought to be made up of quarks and leptons. Quarks form the large baryons and mesons. There are six quarks named up (u), down (d), strange (s), charm (c), bottom (b), and top (t). (The last two are sometimes fancifully referred to as "beauty" and "truth.") Each comes in three "colors" and each has an antiparticle making 36 in all. The six quarks have been confirmed through indirect observations, but not isolated as individual particles.

Refer to the accompanying table of subatomic particles to answer the questions.

Table:

HADRONS - made of quarks

* BARYONS - made of three quarks or three anti-quarks
    NUCLEONS - contain no strange quarks

PARTICLE	CHARGE	MASS(MeV)
proton	1	938.27231
anti-proton	-1	938.27231
neutron	0	939.56563
anti-neutron	0	939.56563

    HYPERONS - contain one or more strange quarks

PARTICLE	CHARGE	MASS(MeV)
lambda	0	1115.684
anti-lambda	0	1115.684
positive sigma	1	1189.37
anti-positive sigma	-1	1189.37
neutral sigma	0	1192.55
anti-neutral sigma	0	1192.55
negative sigma	-1	1197.436
anti-negative sigma	1	1197.436
neutral xi	0	1314.9
anti-neutral xi	0	1314.9
negative xi	-1	1321.32
anti-negative xi	1	1321.32
negative omega	-1	1672.45
positive omega	1	1672.45

* MESONS - made of one quark and one anti-quark

PARTICLE	CHARGE	MASS(MeV)
positive pion	1	139.56995
negative pion	-1	139.56995
neutral pion	0	134.9764
positive kaon	1	493.677
negative kaon	-1	493.677
neutral kaon	0	497.672
anti-neutral kaon	0	497.672
eta	0	547.45

LEPTONS - elementary particles not made of quarks

PARTICLE	CHARGE	MASS(MeV)
positron	1	0.51099907
electron	-1	0.51099907
electron neutrino	0	0
electron anti-neutrino	0	0
positive muon	1	105.658389

negative muon	-1	105.658389
muon neutrino	0	0
muon anti-neutrino	0	0
positive tau	1	1777
negative tau	-1	1777
tau neutrino	0	0
tau anti-neutrino	0	0

17. Which of the following particles has the greatest mass?
    A. Muon
    B. Electron
    C. Proton
    D. Lambda

18. Which of the following particles are made of quarks?
    F. Neutrino
    G. Muon
    H. Proton
    J. None of these

19. When a particle decays, the total charge on the resulting particles must always
    A. be neutral.
    B. be equal to 0.
    C. satisfy the law of conservation of mass.
    D. be equal to the charge of the original particle.

20. The most massive uncharged particles are found among the
    F. Leptons.
    G. Mesons.
    H. Baryons.
    J. Hyperons.

21. A lambda particle decays and one of the products is a proton. A second particle is also formed. Which of the following is the second particle?
    A. Negative pion
    B. Positron
    C. Electron neutrino
    D. Neutron

22. A positive muon decays and one of the products is a positron. If a second particle is also formed, which of the following might it be?
    F. Proton
    G. Tau
    H. Neutrino
    J. Kaon

23. A negative omega particle decays into a lambda particle and a negative kaon. How much energy is released?
    A. 63.09 MeV
    B. 1115.68 MeV
    C. 493.68 MeV
    D. 1672.45 MeV

24. Tom weighs 60 kilograms. What is his mass in MeV?
    F. 6×10^{11}
    G. 33.65×10^{30}
    H. 60
    J. Cannot be determined

Questions 25-32 pertain to the following information:

Pollutants typically enter seawater at *point sources*, such as sewage discharge pipes or factory waste outlets. Then, they may be spread over a wide area by wave action and currents. The rate of this dispersal depends upon a number of factors, including depth, temperature, and the speed of the currents. Chemical pollutants often attach themselves to small particles of sediment, so that studying the dispersal of sediment can help in understanding how pollution spreads.

In a study of this type, a team of scientists lowered screened collection vessels to various depths to collect particles of different sizes. This gave them an idea of the size distribution of particles at each depth. Figure A shows the results for six different sites (ND, NS, MD, MS, SD, and SS). The particle size is plotted in *phi* units, which is a logarithmic scale used to measure grain sizes of sand and gravel. The 0 point of the scale is a grain size of 1 millimeter, and an increase of 1 in phi number corresponds to a decrease in grain size by a factor of ½, so that 1 phi unit is a grain size of 0.5 mm, 2 phi units is 0.25 mm, and so on; in the other direction, -1 phi unit corresponds to a grain size of 2 mm and -2 phi units to 4 mm.

Grains of different size are carried at different rates by the currents in the water. The study also measured current speed and direction, pressure and temperature at different depths, and at different times of year. The results were used in a computer *modeling program* to predict the total transport of sediments both along the shore (north-south) and perpendicular to it (east-west). Figure B shows the program's calculation of the distance particles would have been transported during the study period. The abbreviation *mab* in the figure stands for *meters above bottom*.

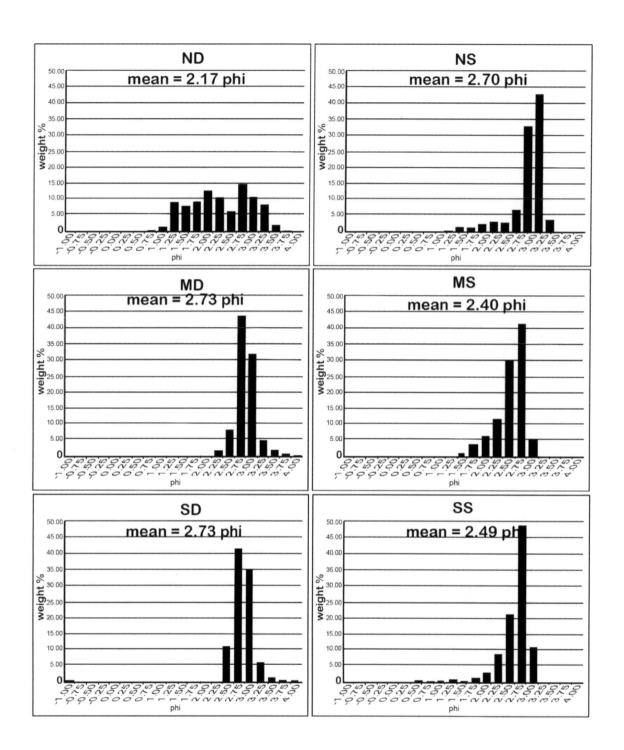

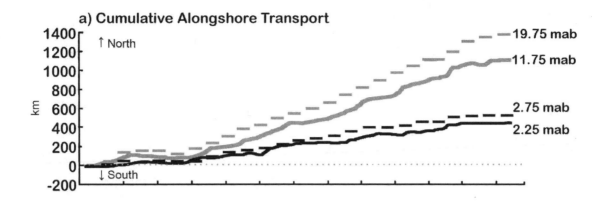

a) Cumulative Alongshore Transport

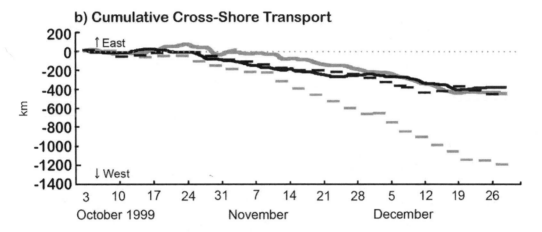

b) Cumulative Cross-Shore Transport

25. Which of the following sites was found to have the smallest average particle size?
    A. ND
    B. NS
    C. MD
    D. MS

26. With the exception of a few outliers, all of the phi values were in the range 1.0 to 4.0. This means that
    F. All particles studied were smaller than 0.5 mm.
    G. All particles studied were between 1.0 and 4.0 mm.
    H. No screens larger than 4.0 m were used in the study.
    J. All particles were larger than 0.5 mm.

27. For which site is it *least* true that the mean particle size represents the entire population?
    A. ND
    B. NS
    C. MD
    D. MS

28. What particle size corresponds to a phi value of -3?
    F. 2mm
    G. 0.5 mm
    H. 0.0625 mm
    J. 8 mm

29. In Figure B, the absolute value of the slope of the curves corresponds to
    A. The speed of transport.
    B. The size of the particles.
    C. The phi value.
    D. The depth.

30. The data indicates that along a NS axis
    F. Transport is faster in deeper waters.
    G. Transport is faster in shallower waters.
    H. Transport is the same at all depths.
    J. There is no correlation between transport speed and depth.

31. The data indicates that along the EW axis
    A. Transport is faster in deeper waters.
    B. Transport is faster in shallower waters.
    C. Transport is the same at all depths.
    D. There is no correlation between transport speed and depth.

32. Which of the following is closest to the overall direction of transport?
    F. N
    G. NW
    H. NE
    J. SE

Questions 33-40 pertain to the following passage:

Wind can provide a renewable source of energy. The energy of the wind is actually solar energy, as the sun warms the Earth's surface by varying amounts at different locations. This creates differential pressures as the warm air expands, and initiates air motions. High altitude airflows are similar to ocean currents, but near the surface, winds are affected by surface features.

Wind turbines capture this energy with a set of rotors that are set into rotation by the wind. The rotors are made of lightweight fiberglass or carbon fiber, and are held aloft on a tall tower. It is important to hold the blades high above the ground to avoid wind shear, a difference in airflow at different points along the rotor blades which can damage them. The blades rotate at about 40 rpm. Through a gearbox, they rotate a driveshaft at about 1500 rpm. The shaft, in turn, drives a generator.

The power P available from moving air is proportional to the cube of the wind velocity:

$$P = \frac{1}{2}\rho A v^3$$

where$A$ is the cross section covered by the blades, ρ is the air density, and v is the air velocity. As the air passes through the rotor, it slows down. The turbine cannot take all the energy from the air, since then it would stop dead behind the rotor. Theoretically, the maximum efficiency that can be achieved is 59%. Figures A and B show a power curve for a 600 kilowatt (kW) wind turbine. To avoid damage from excessive winds, starting with wind speeds of 15 m/sec, the blades are adjusted to limit the power to 600 kW. For winds above 25 m/sec, the turbine is shut down.

One drawback of wind turbines has been the noise they make, but modern designs with slow-rotating blades are fairly quiet. Figure C shows the noise spectrum of a large turbine. The x-axis shows the frequency of sound in Hertz, and the y-axis shows the level of sound at each frequency. The total noise is 50 decibels (dB), which is less than the noise in a typical office.

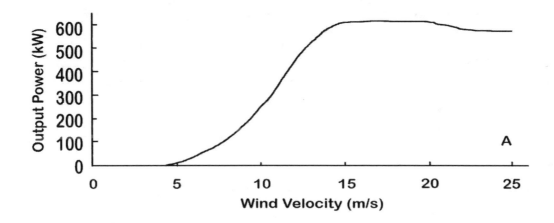

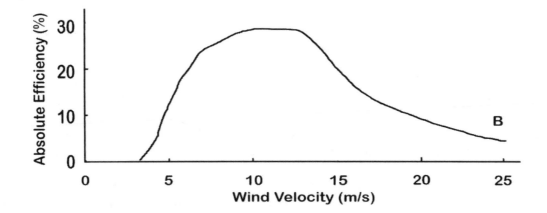

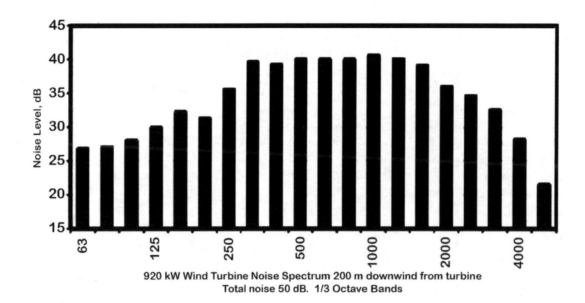

920 kW Wind Turbine Noise Spectrum 200 m downwind from turbine
Total noise 50 dB. 1/3 Octave Bands

33. What wind velocity provides the maximum efficiency for this turbine?
    A. 5 m/s
    B. 7 m/s
    C. 10 m/s
    D. 12 m/s

34. What wind velocity provides the maximum power output from this turbine?
    F. 5 m/s
    G. 7 m/s
    H. 10 m/s
    J. 15 m/s

35. Why does the curve in Figure A flatten for wind velocities greater than 15 m/sec?
    A. The generator runs less efficiently.
    B. The rotors are being trimmed to prevent damage.
    C. Surface turbulence makes the rotors turn more slowly.
    D. None of the above.

36. For wind speeds between 5 and 10 m/sec, we expect the curve in Figure A to increase
    F. Linearly
    G. Irregularly
    H. Exponentially
    J. Sinusoidally

37. An ideal wind turbine operates at 100% efficiency and generates 200 kW of power at a wind velocity of 6 m/sec. How much power will be available at a wind velocity of 12 m/sec?
    A. 400 kW
    B. 800 kW
    C. 1200 kW
    D. 1600 kW

38. A wind turbine operating at 50% efficiency generates 100 kW of power at a wind velocity of 6 m/sec. If it also works at 50% efficiency at winds of 12 m/sec, how much power will it generate?

    F. 400 kW

    G. 800 kW

    H. 1200 kW

    J. 1600 kW

39. Figure C shows that

    A. Most of the noise is at high frequencies.

    B. Most of the noise is at low frequencies.

    C. Most of the noise is at middle frequencies.

    D. The total noise is less than 40 dB.

40. The energy captured by wind turbines is created by

    F. Surface features.

    G. Carbon fiber materials.

    H. A generator.

    J. The sun.

Writing

Merit pay for teachers is the practice of giving increased pay based upon the improvement in student performance. It is a controversial idea among educators and policy makers. Those who support this idea say that, with it, school districts are able to select and retain the best teachers and to improve student performance. Others argue that merit pay systems lead to teacher competition for the best students and to test-driven teaching practices that are detrimental to the overall quality of education.

In your essay, select either of these points of view, or suggest an alternative approach, and make a case for it. Use specific reasons and appropriate examples to support your position and to show how it is superior to the others.

Answer Key and Explanations

English

Number	Answer	Number	Answer	Number	Answer
1	B	26	J	51	A
2	G	27	B	52	J
3	A	28	H	53	C
4	G	29	C	54	H
5	C	30	H	55	B
6	F	31	C	56	H
7	C	32	H	57	B
8	G	33	C	58	H
9	B	34	J	59	D
10	J	35	B	60	H
11	C	36	F	61	C
12	J	37	B	62	G
13	B	38	H	63	B
14	G	39	D	64	J
15	B	40	G	65	D
16	H	41	B	66	H
17	D	42	H	67	A
18	G	43	D	68	H
19	B	44	G	69	B
20	G	45	D	70	H
21	A	46	F	71	B
22	F	47	B	72	J
23	B	48	H	73	B
24	G	49	B	74	H
25	B	50	H	75	A

1. B: The rest of the paragraph is written in the past tense. The other choices are all present tense.

2. G: The author wishes to emphasize that the area where the Wampanoag lived was not called Massachusetts at that time. The other choices do not do that.

3. A: This is an example of an introductory word coming before the main clause and set off by a comma, for emphasis. Answers B and D differ in meaning from the original text.

4. G: The expression joins an independent clause to a dependent one, so a comma is not required. Answers F and H are redundant, since "and" and "also" have similar meaning.

5. C: No verb follows "animals" which, like "forest" is an indirect object, so no comma is needed. Answer B is needlessly wordy.

6. F: This is the possessive pronoun. The sentence makes no sense with any of the other spellings.

7. C: This gives the sentence a parallel construction of elements that modify the noun "stories." Answer A is grammatically correct but reads with less clarity.

8. G: This is the most specific as well as the simplest. While the statement may be true for Indians in general, the article is about the Wampanoag.

9. B: The clause beginning in "but" is independent, so that a comma is required.

10. J: The original sentence includes two independent clauses, which must be separated by a comma and one of seven coordinating conjunctions: and, but, for, or, nor, so, yet. Alternatively, they may be split into two sentences, as is done for answer J. Answer G contains the redundancy "and…also."

11. C: The elements of a list require separation by commas.

12. J: This gives a construction parallel to "from land".

13. B: This causes the verb "growing" to be compared to "hunting" rather than to the noun "animals." As written, the sentence implies that the animals were grown.

14. G: The phrase is completely unnecessary to understand the meaning of the sentence.

15. B

16. H: In the original text, the word "would" is slang and adds nothing to the sentence. Answers G and J differ in meaning from the original.

17. D: The hyphens clarify the meaning by showing that the entire three-word clause modifies the expression "food supply."

18. G: By separating the modifying clause "in recent years," it clarifies the meaning of the sentence.

19. B: The original does not specify who is referred to by the word "their," which is unnecessary. Answer D is is incorrect usage.

20. G: The word "that" has already appeared ("you would think that...") and is redundant if used again here.

21. A: None of the other spellings make sense in this usage.

22. F: The percentage plainly refers to the population mentioned earlier in the sentence. All the other answers are redundant.

23. B: This is the possessive of a plural noun. The original text offers the possessive of a singular noun, which is incorrect. The other answers are not possessives.

24. G: This is also the simplest. The word "still" in the original suggests that people will not buy expensive foods even if some other condition is met, but no such condition is specified. Therefore, the word is unnecessary and confusing.

25. B: The word "your" in the original is slang usage. Answer C is incorrect because it is a plural, not a possessive.

26. J: In this case, "too" means "also."

27. B: The phrase is redundant since the word "theory" is included in the name "the paycheck cycle theory" which follows immediately afterwards in the sentence.

28. H: The word "family" is used redundantly in the original sentence, and is easily replaced by a pronoun in this case.

29. C: The hypothesis suggests the existence of a cycle that promotes weight gain. In the original, the word "that" makes the sentence nonsensical.

30. H: The use of "would" in the original is slang. The author is saying that, if the paycheck cycle hypothesis is correct, the two causes of overweight are periodic food restriction and poor diet. Since there is some uncertainty here, H is a better choice than G.

31. C: This is the possessive of the plural noun "women."

32. H: This is a possessive. Answer J is technically correct, but it is common usage to use this expression as a collective noun, so that "porter's lodge" can describe a lodge for more than one porter.

33. C: The other answers do not make sense.

34. J: The original text's "accesses" requires a singular subject.

35. B: Answer C changes the meaning, suggesting that the action is not performed every day, whereas the original text indicates that it occurs daily but that the time is indefinite.

36. F: "Entryway" is the correct spelling.

37. B: The phrase in the original is unnecessary, and is redundant as it repeats "only." The other answers are unnecessarily wordy.

38. H: The original text splits the infinitive "to receive." Answers G and J imply that this happens all the time, whereas the text implies that it is an exceptional occurrence.

39. D: Answer C repeats the word "even" and is redundant.

40. G: The original text is phrased awkwardly, and answers H and J change the meaning.

41. B: This provides a parallel construction between "morning" and "evening."

42. H: The original seeks to imply that the guards are not effectively on watch, but the phrasing is awkward and makes no sense. Answer G is correctly spelled, but retains the awkward phrasing of the original.

43. D: Since all the elements of the list contain verbs, this choice provides for parallel construction by also including the verb. Answer C is less desirable since the phrase "physically out of shape" is redundant.

44. G: The other choices are unnecessarily wordy.

45. D: which most specifically explains what has been ineffective about the tactics of the guards. Answer C is vague.

46. F: Capitalization is required since the school name is a proper noun, and a possessive is needed since the program belongs to the school.

47. B: The infinitive ("to do") should always be used in the present tense.

48. H: The infinitive ("to afford") should always be used in the present tense.

49. B: The original is redundant, since "at last" and "finally" have the same meaning.

50. H: The original version is awkward, since it repeats the word "soon" which appeared earlier in the same sentence.

51. A: The comma is not required before a subordinating conjunction such as "until."

52. J: The commas are used to set off Dr. Ed Cook's name as a parenthetical element.

53. C: In the original version, the word "this" is slang usage.

54. H: The original version is nonsensical, and none of the other answers are grammatically correct.

55. B: Answer C is grammatically correct, but the phrase adds nothing to the author's description of the purpose of the work done on board the boat.

56. H: The original version is needlessly wordy, and both it and answer G contain the assumption that the tests will be successful. Answers H and J are more precise in that they do not make this assumption, but J repeats the word "test", so that H is the better choice.

57. B: In the original version, "these" is slang usage. Answers C and D are grammatically correct but needlessly vague.

58. H: This sentence is completely unrelated to the material that precedes it in the paragraph, which warrants beginning a new one.

59. D: This is an example of slang usage and is exceedingly vague. If the author wanted to indicate that the fish were interested in the ship's lights and in other things, as well, one or more examples should have been given.

60. H: This provides the same information as the other choices but is far more concise.

61. C: As this phrase tells the reader where the man appeared. Answer A creates a run-on sentence, answer B is redundant, and choice D creates a disagreement of verb tense.

62. G: The original and answer H are slang usage, and J, suggesting that the villagers had only then noticed the monkeys, is inappropriate.

63. B: As the clause following the conjunction and is dependent, the comma is not employed.

64. J: The action described in the portion of the sentence following the conjunction is contrary to expectation, since the villagers hunted less despite the generous payments, and but reflects that contradiction better than any of the other choices.

65. D: The correct spelling for the possessive pronoun.

66. H: This implies that the action that follows is a consequence of the one that precedes, i.e., the man raised his price because the villagers were losing interest.

67. A: No comma is used to set off a dependent clause.

68. H: This is an adjective indicating finite supply. Answer F is an adverb, inappropriate for modifying a noun.

69. B: This avoids splitting the infinitive "to see" while maintaining the emphasis provided by "even."

70. H: This proper use of the infinitive also maintains parallel structure with "to see," which appears earlier in the same sentence.

71. B: A semi-colon may be used to join two sentences when they are of similar content.

72. J: This uses the subjective pronoun he with the verb to be. Answers G and H create a repetitive structure within the paragraph.

73. B: This uses the subjective pronoun I with the verb to be.

74. H: The past tense is needed since the story is set in the past. Answer J is slang usage.

75. A: The comma appropriately sets off the ending clause and adds emphasis. Answer B is a run-on sentence, while C and D introduce changes in meaning.

Mathematics

Number	Answer	Number	Answer	Number	Answer
1	C	21	D	41	E
2	H	22	F	42	J
3	B	23	E	43	B
4	K	24	G	44	G
5	A	25	B	45	C
6	J	26	K	46	G
7	D	27	C	47	A
8	F	28	K	48	H
9	A	29	B	49	B
10	J	30	G	50	J
11	E	31	A	51	E
12	F	32	G	52	F
13	B	33	A	53	C
14	H	34	G	54	G
15	A	35	A	55	C
16	G	36	H	56	G
17	A	37	D	57	B
18	G	38	K	58	J
19	C	39	A	59	B
20	F	40	F	60	F

1. C: $6\sqrt{10} = \sqrt{6^2} \times \sqrt{10} = \sqrt{36} \times \sqrt{10} = \sqrt{360}$.

2. H: $16.5 \times \dfrac{4}{3} = 22$.

3. B: The equation $y = -3x + 2$ has a negative slope (-3), and a positive intercept (+2).

4. K: The fraction of students who play drums plus the fraction of those who play a brass instrument must total 1. So, the number of students who play drums is pn, and the number who play brass must be $(1-p)n$.

5. A: This is a right triangle, since the two angles shown add up to 90 degrees, and the remaining angle must therefore be 90 degrees. For a right triangle, the length of a side is related to the hypotenuse by the sine of the opposite angle. Thus, $A = C\sin(30^o)$, and since the sine of a 30-degree angle is 0.5, $A = C/2$.

6. J: An easy way to do this is to remember that for a number to be divisible by 3, the sum of the digits must be divisible by 3. Thus, for 555, $5+5+5=15$, and $15 \div 3 = 5$. Likewise, $555 \div 3 = 185$.

7. D: Distance is the product of velocity and time, and $(5 \times 10^6) \times 2 \times 10^{-4} = (10 \times 10^6 \times 10^{-4})$ $= 10^3 = 1000$.

8. F: Since the second line, $y = 3$, is horizontal, the intersection must occur at a point where $y = 3$. If $x = -1.5$, the equation describing the line is satisfied: $(2 \times [-1.5] + 3) = 0$.

9. A: For the line to be parallel to the x-axis, the slope must be 0. This condition is met if y has a constant value.

10. J: The radius r of this circle is the line OA. Since B is a right angle, OA is the hypotenuse, and by the Pythagorean Theorem, $r^2 = x^2 + y^2$, so that $r = \sqrt{x^2 + y^2}$.

11. E: If segment AB equals segment OB, then the tangent of the $\angle AOB$ must be 1 ($\tan(AOB) = \dfrac{AB}{OB} = 1$), which is the tangent of a 45 degree angle. Further, since AOB is a right triangle with $\angle ABO$ = 90 degrees, and since the sum of the angles in a triangle must equal 180 degrees, $\angle BAO$ must also be 45 degrees ($45 + 45 + 90 = 180$). Therefore, A and B are both correct.

12. F: Since OA and OC are both radii of the same circle, they must be equal.

13. B: 25% off is equivalent to $25 \times \dfrac{\$138}{100} = \$34.50$, so the sale price becomes $138 - $34.50 = $103.50.

14. H: The expression 2^{-3} is equivalent to $\dfrac{1}{2^3}$, and since $2^3 = 8$, it is equivalent to 1/8.

15. A: As defined, the line will be described by the equation $y = 4x + 1$. Expression A fits this equation ($9 = 4 \times 2 + 1$). The others do not.

16. G: 30% 0f 3300 = 0.3 x 3300 = 990.

17. A: The vertical operators indicate absolute values, which are always positive. Thus, | 7 – 5 | = 2, and | 5 – 7 | = | -2 | = 2, and 2 – 2 = 0.

18. G: The value of the fraction, $\dfrac{7}{5}$, can be evaluated by dividing 7 by 5, which yields 1.4. The average of 1.4 and 1.4 is $\dfrac{1.4 + 1.4}{2} = 1.4$.

19. C: The surface of a cube is obtained by multiplying the area of each face by 6, since there are 6 faces. The area of each face is the square of the length of one edge. Therefore, $A = 6 \times 3^2 = 6 \times 9 = 54$.

20. F: The area A of a circle is given by $A = \pi \times r^2$, where r is the radius. Since π is approximately 3.14, we can solve for $r = \sqrt{\dfrac{A}{\pi}} = \sqrt{\dfrac{314}{3.14}} = \sqrt{100} = 10$. Now, the diameter d is twice the radius, or $d = 2 \times 10 = 20$.

21. D: Inspection of the data shows that the distance traveled by the car during any 1-unit interval (velocity) is 20 units. However, the first data point shows that the car is 50 units from the point of origin at time 2, so it had a 10-unit head-start before time measurement began.

22. F: The perimeter of a circle is given by $2\pi r$, where r is the radius. We solve for $r = \dfrac{35}{2\pi} = 5.57$, and double this value to obtain the diameter: $d = 11.14$ feet.

23. E: The sum of angles in a triangle equals 180 degrees. Therefore, solve for the remaining angle: $180 - (15 + 70) = 95$ degrees.

24. G: This answer may be determined using the Law of Sines, which relates the sides of a triangle and their opposing angles as follows:

$$\frac{a}{\sin A} = \frac{b}{\sin B} = \frac{c}{\sin C}$$

Thus, we have $\sin A = a \times \dfrac{\sin B}{b} = 14 \times \dfrac{\sin(35)}{12} = 14 \times \dfrac{0.57}{12} = 0.67$, and $\sin^{-1}(0.67) = 42$ degrees.

25. B: The inequality specifies that the difference between L and 15 inches must be less or equal to 0.01. For choice B, $| 14.99 - 15 | = | -0.01 | = 0.01$, which is equal to the specified tolerance, and therefore meets the condition.

26. K: The product of x and $\dfrac{1}{x}$ is $\dfrac{1}{x} \times x = \dfrac{x}{x} = 1$. The expression x^{-1} is equivalent to $\dfrac{1}{x}$.

27. C: The total distance traveled was $8 + 3.6 = 11.6$ miles. The first 1/5 of a mile is charged at the higher rate. Since $1/5 = 0.2$, the remainder of the trip is 11.4 miles. Thus, the fare for the distance traveled is computed as $\$5.50 + 5 \times 11.4 \times \$1.50 = \$91$. To this, the charge for waiting time must be added, which is simply 9 x 20¢ = 180¢ = $1.80. Finally, add the two charges, $91 + $1.80 = $92.80.

28. K: Each term of each expression in parentheses must be multiplied by each term in the other. Thus for K, $(x + 3)(3x - 5) = 3x^2 + 9x - 5x - 15 = 3x^2 + 4x - 15$.

29. B: First, determine the proportion of students in the fifth grade. Since the total number of students is 180, this proportion is $\dfrac{36}{180} = 0.2$, or 20%. Next, determine the same proportion of the total prizes, which is 20% of twenty, or $0.2 \times 20 = 4$.

30. G: The probability of playing a song by any band is proportional to the number of songs by that band, divided by the total number of songs, or $\frac{5}{15} = \frac{1}{3}$ for Band D. The probability of playing any particular song is not affected by what has been played previously, since the choice is random.

31. A: Since 3 of the 15 songs are by Band B, the probability that any one song will be by that band is $\frac{3}{15} = \frac{1}{5}$. The probability that two successive events will occur is the product of the probabilities for any one event or, in this case $\frac{1}{5} \times \frac{1}{5} = \frac{1}{25}$.

32. G: A prime number is a natural, positive, non-zero number that can only be factored by itself and 1. This is the case for 11.

33. A: From the starting expression, compute as follows:
$$3(\frac{6x-3}{3}) - 3(9x+9) = 3(2x-1) - 27x - 27 = 6x - 3 - 27x - 27 = -21x - 30 = -3(7x+10).$$

34. G: Compute as follows: $(3 - 2 \times 2)^2 = (3 - 4)^2 = (-1)^2 = 1$.

35. A: This is evident if the line EG is drawn parallel to segment BD,

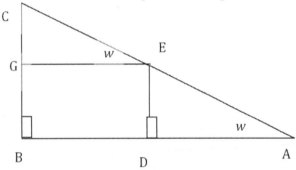

First, note that if AB is twice the length of AD, then it follows that AB is also twice the length of DB (AB = 2 DB), since AB = AD + DB. It can be seen that angle w at the vertex E is the same as the angle w at vertex A, so that the cosines of these two angles must be the same. This gives $\frac{AB}{AC} = \frac{EG}{EC}$, and since DB = EG, it follows that $\frac{AB}{AC} = \frac{DB}{EC}$, which is equivalent to $\frac{AC}{AB} = \frac{EC}{DB}$. Now, since AB = 2 DB, $\frac{AC}{2 \times DB} = \frac{EC}{DB}$. By rearranging the equality, $EC = \frac{DB \times AC}{2 \times DB}$, and then simplifying, we get $EC = \frac{AC}{2}$, or AC = 2 EC.

36. H: The side of the square is equal to the diameter of the circle, or twice the radius, or $2r$. The area of the square is this quantity squared, or $4r^2$. The area of the circle is πr^2.

Subtracting the area of the circle from the area of the square gives the difference between the two areas:
$\Delta A = 4r^2 - \pi r^2 = r^2(4-\pi)$.

37. D: The vertical sides of the rectangle are equal to $2r$, where r is the radius of the circles (see Figure). Similarly, the horizontal side of the rectangle is equal to $4r$. Thus, the area of the rectangle is $A_R = 2r \times 4r = 8r^2$. If this equals 32 square meters, as given, then solve for r:

$$8r^2 = 32$$
$$r^2 = \frac{32}{8} = 4$$

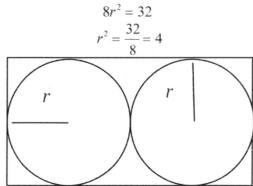

so that $r = \sqrt{4} = 2$. Therefore, the area of a circle, $A_C = \pi r^2 = 4\pi$.

38. K: The weight of the ball, W, is the product of the density, d, and the volume, V. Since a ball is a sphere, and the radius is half of the diameter, the volume is $V = \frac{4}{3}\pi r^3$, so that

$$W = d \times \frac{4}{3}\pi r^3 = 4 \times \frac{4}{3}\pi \times 3^3 = d \times \frac{4}{3}\pi \times 27 = 452.16\,\text{gm}.$$

39. A: The difference in densities between cork and normal fill for the ball is $4 - 3 = 1$ gm/cm^3. The actual ball weighs $452.16 - 413.38 = 38.78$ gm less than expected (ΔW). Therefore there is a sphere within the ball that weighs 38.78 gm less than expected. Since the difference in densities, Δd, is 1, the volume of that sphere is determined as
$$\Delta W = \Delta d \times \frac{4}{3}\pi r^3.$$
Solving for r,
$$r^3 = \frac{\Delta W}{\Delta d} \times \frac{3}{4\pi} = \frac{38.78}{1} \times \frac{3}{4\pi} = 9.26, \text{ and}$$

$$r = \sqrt[3]{9.26} = 2.10\,\text{cm}.$$

40. F: Each glass of lemonade costs 10¢, or \$0.10, so that g glasses will cost $g \times \$0.10$. To this, add Bob's fixed cost of \$45, giving the expression in F.

41. E: Evaluate as follows:
$$(3x^{-2})^3 = 3^3 \times (x^{-2})^3 = 27 \times \left(\frac{1}{x^2}\right)^3 = 27 \times \frac{1}{x^6} = 27x^{-6}$$

42. J: Let P_A = the price of truck A, and P_B = the price of truck B. Similarly let M_A and M_B represent the gas mileage obtained by each truck. The total cost of driving a truck n miles is

$$C = P + n \times \frac{\$4}{M}.$$

To determine the break-even mileage, set the two cost equations equal to one another and solve for n:

$$P_A + n \times \frac{\$4}{M_A} = P_B + n \times \frac{\$4}{M_B}$$

$$n \times (\frac{\$4}{M_A} - \frac{\$4}{M_B}) = P_B - P_A$$

$$n = \frac{P_B - P_A}{(\frac{\$4}{M_A} - \frac{\$4}{M_B})}$$

Plugging in the given values,

$$n = \frac{650 - 450}{(\frac{4}{25} - \frac{4}{35})} = \frac{200}{(0.16 - 0.1143)} = 4375 \text{ miles.}$$

43. B: The lowest score, 72, is eliminated. The average of the remaining four grades is

$$Avg = \frac{75 + 88 + 86 + 90}{4} = 84.75.$$

Rounding up to the nearest integer gives a final grade of 85.

44. G: To calculate S, first calculate the discount, and then subtract it from the original price, p. In this case, the discount is 33% of p, or 0.33p. Thus, $S = p - 0.33p$.

45. C: The volume of a right, circular cylinder is equal to its height multiplied by the area of its base, A. Since the base is circular, $A = \pi R^2$, where R, the radius, is half of the diameter, or 30 feet. Therefore,

$$V = H \times \pi R^2$$

Solving for H,

$$H = \frac{V}{\pi R^2} = \frac{1,000,000}{\pi \times 30^2} = \frac{1,000,000}{\pi \times 900} = 353.86 \text{ ft.}$$

46. G: Simply evaluating the expression yields

$$y(15) = -\frac{1}{2}(32)(15)^2 + 0 + 30,000 = -\frac{1}{2}(32)(225) + 0 + 30,000 = -3,600 + 30,000$$
$$= 26,400 \text{ ft.}$$

47. A: The sine function is a periodic function whose value oscillates between 1 and -1, just as Curve #1 does.

48. H: The equation can be presented with x as the independent variable by rearranging, since $x = y - 1$ is equivalent to
$$y = x + 1,$$
which is the equation for a straight line of slope 1 and intercept 1, just like Curve #3.

49. B: The equation can be presented with x as the independent variable by solving for y, since $x = \sqrt{y}$ is equivalent to
$$y = x^2,$$
which is an exponential equation that increases more and more rapidly with x.

    Note: In the form given, $x = \sqrt{y}$, the function gives rise to no negative values of x.

50. J: The equation can be presented with x as the independent variable by rearranging, since $x = y + 1$ is equivalent to
$$y = x - 1,$$
which is the equation for a straight line of slope 1 and intercept -1, just like Curve #4.

51. E: The equation can be presented with x as the independent variable by solving for y, since $x = y^2$ is equivalent to
$$y = \sqrt{x},$$
which is an equation that returns two values of y for each value of x, and is not defined for negative values of x.

52. F: The band's share, 25% of \$20,000,000, is \$5,000,000. After the agent's share is subtracted, the band gets $(1 - 0.15) \times \$5,000,000 = 0.85 \times \$5,000,000 = \$4,250,000$, and each band member gets one fifth of that, or \$850,000.

53. C: Rearranging the equation gives
$3(y + 4) = 15(y - 5)$, which is equivalent to
$15y - 3y = 12 + 75$, or
$12y = 87$, and solving for y yields
$$y = \frac{87}{12} = \frac{29}{4}.$$

54. G: Rearranging each equation so that it shows y as a function of the variable x, we have
$$y = -\frac{a}{3}x + \frac{18}{3} \text{ and } y = -\frac{15}{a}x + \frac{24}{a}.$$
The lines will be parallel if the slopes, or the terms factoring x, are equal. Therefore,
$-\frac{a}{3} = -\frac{15}{a}$, which yields $a^2 = 45$, and taking the square root, yields
$$a = \sqrt{45}.$$

55. C: The percentage of students not wearing hats is simply 100% - p%. Since percentage means "parts per hundred", the fraction not wearing hats is $\dfrac{100-p}{100}$, and this fraction is multiplied by the number of students.

56. G: Distance traveled is the product of velocity and time, or
$D = 3 \times 10^{-11} \times 1 \times 10^{6} = (3 \times 1) \times (10^{-11} \times 10^{6}) = 3 \times 10^{-5}$ meters.

57. B: The median is the value in a group of numbers that separates the upper-half from the lower-half, so that there are an equal number of values above and below it. In this distribution, there are two values greater than 116, and two values below it.

58. J: The product $(a)(a)(a)(a)(a)$ is defined as a to the fifth power.

59. B: $7.5 \times 10^{-4} = \dfrac{7.5}{10,000} = 0.00075$.

60. F: Rearranging the equation gives $x^2 = -1$. However, the square of a real number cannot yield a negative result, so no real number solutions exist for the equation.

Reading

Number	Answer	Number	Answer
1	C	21	D
2	G	22	H
3	B	23	B
4	J	24	H
5	C	25	D
6	G	26	F
7	A	27	C
8	F	28	G
9	D	29	B
10	G	30	G
11	B	31	B
12	G	32	F
13	C	33	C
14	H	34	G
15	B	35	B
16	H	36	H
17	B	37	B
18	H	38	J
19	B	39	D
20	F	40	G

1. C: The passage makes no mention of metals or horses. Although we may infer that they hunted the buffalo because they were plentiful, that is not stated in the passage.

2. G: Travail means work, or effort, and shows that the crows made it more difficult for the people to kill buffalo during the hunt.

3. B: The story tells us that after the great white crow turned black, all the other crows were black as well. Thus, he is a symbol for all these birds.

4. J: Line 18 tells us that the tribe planned to frighten the chief of the crows to prevent the crows from warning the buffalo about the hunts. The passage does not suggest that they hated all birds or that they planned to eat this one.

5. C: Long Arrow acted like the buffalo in the herd so that the chief of the crows would approach, making it possible to capture him. Although we may infer that he had to fool the buffalo in the herd as well, this is secondary to his need to fool the birds.

6. G: These details help us to see how the people lived. Although they hunted with the stone-tipped spears, the rawhide bag was not a part of the hunt.

7. A: As he lands, he asks "have you not heard my warning?" (Line 41).

8. F: The suggestions included several for killing or mutilating the bird, which does not suggest a calm resolve. And there is no suggestion that they were either celebrating or hungry at this time.

9. D: There is no characterization of Long Arrow in the passage, and we know nothing about him or why he was chosen.

10. G: The birds in the story are able to observe the actions of hunters, to interpret them as potentially harmful for their buffalo friends, and to act for the protection of the buffalo. They do not appear to do this for their own benefit, nor do they seem to act specifically to harm the tribe, but rather to help the buffalo.

11. B: The first paragraph refers to the Spray as a sloop, which is a kind of sailboat, and refers to its being berthed among the docks.

12. G: In the first paragraph the author describes his surprise at the changes in the harbor, and in Lines 8-10 indicates that the changes downtown were much less.

13. C: Lines 10 mentions a letter of introduction that had been sent ahead from another of the author's contacts in Montevideo.

14. H: Line 15 mentions the "Standard's" columns, which had contained stories about the Spray's voyage.

15. B: Although "landmarks" are usually monuments or buildings, the author uses the term and goes on to describe a number of merchants who had been present during his earlier visit to the city, and who were significant features of the town in his estimation.

16. H: Line 22 tells us that the lemons "went on forever," suggesting that the merchant hardly ever changed them at all.

17. B: The author would have liked to look up the whiskey merchant, but there is nothing in the passage to suggest that he was desperate or anxious to do so.

18. H: The phrase in Line 32, that the waters were not blameless of disease germs, indicates that some germs may have been present in them.

19. B: Throughout the passage, the author is looking for people he had seen on his first visit, and he says of this merchant that he had "survived" (Line 35).

20. F: Since the sign has been present since the author's previous visit to the city, we may infer that the merchant is not really concerned about an imminent comet strike. And the wording of the sign suggests that his wares are for sale "at any price" (Line 37).

21. D: Choices A-C all have similar meanings and match the text's description of Lubitsch's film style as elegant or sophisticated.

22. H: This phrase is used in the last sentence to describe the Lubitsch style.

23. B: Lubitsch's focus on seemingly irrelevant details as symbols is described in the text as his signature style (Line 14)

24. H: Lubitsch was invited in 1923 by Albert Zukor (Line 12).

25. D: Made in 1912, the film could not have been a talkie, as it was not until 1923 that Lubitsch went to Hollywood to use sound technology. And the text tells us nothing of the film's content or personnel.

26. F:Monescu and Lily were both thieves who posed as members of high society. Mariette was a real heiress, and Lubitsch, of course, was a director, not a character in the film.

27. C: This, indeed, is the underlying theme of the entire movie, as shown by the characters of Monescu and Lily, who appear to be elegant but are, in fact, thieves.

28. G: Lily has no wealth of her own, but Monescu finally chooses her over Mariette and her fortune (Lines 42-43)

29. B: Lily passes herself of as a countess and Montescu poses as a baron (Line 39).

30. G: Line 49 tells us that he made films in English, German, and French, suggesting that part of his film career was spent in France.

31. B: Cilia and flagella are both organelles, which are defined in Line 2 as sub-cellular structures that perform a particular function.

32. F: Line 16 describes the function of cilia as providing fluid flow across the gills or the epithelia lining the digestive tract. The stomach is part of the digestive tract.

33. C: The third paragraph of the text describes 9 peripheral pairs of polymers, and two central ones, or 20 in all.

34. G: Tubulin and dynein are both defined as proteins in the text (Lines 21 and 29). Flagellin is a protein, but it is not mentioned in the text. Sonneborn is not a protein; he was a scientist.

35. B: The mechanism is described in detail in the fourth paragraph. Dynein causes the outer polymer pairs to slide past each other, not to bend. The inner polymers do not have dynein associated with them, so they are not involved in the bending. And the passage cites no evidence to suggest that the organelles contract.

36. H: Although the polymers in this passage are made of protein subunits, the definition (Lines 19-20) is more general. Line 21 tells us that in this case the subunits are tubulin proteins.

37. B: See Line 38.

38. J: The experiment described in Lines 40-44 showed that the cilia always retained their original direction of rotation.

39. D: See Line 7.

40. G: Sonneborn performed his experiment with cilia, not with flagella.

Science

Number	Answer	Number	Answer
1	A	21	A
2	J	22	H
3	C	23	A
4	J	24	G
5	D	25	C
6	J	26	J
7	D	27	A
8	J	28	J
9	A	29	A
10	J	30	G
11	C	31	B
12	G	32	G
13	D	33	C
14	J	34	J
15	B	35	B
16	H	36	H
17	D	37	D
18	H	38	G
19	D	39	C
20	J	40	J

1. A: The peak for albumin is the highest in the electropherogram, so the concentration of albumin is higher than that of any other component.

2. J: The peak for component γ is furthest from the origin along the mobility axis, indicating that it has moved the furthest during the experiment.

3. C: The peak for component $\alpha 1$ lies to the right of that for albumin, indicating greater mobility, and to the right of all the other peaks, indicating lesser mobility than the components represented by those peaks. Since small molecules move faster than large ones, $\alpha 1$ must be smaller than albumin and larger than the other components.

4. J: The peak for component γ is the fastest, indicating that γ is the smallest component seen on the electropherogram.

5. D: The peak for the unknown lies between those for γ and β, indicating an intermediate size. It has moved more rapidly than all components except for component γ.

6. J: If the unknown is an aggregate, it must be larger than the components that have clumped together to form it, not smaller.

7. D: If the unknown is a breakdown product, it must be smaller than the components that have broken down to form it, not larger.

8. J: The experiment shows only that this patient's blood contains an unknown component. It does not demonstrate that the component causes the patient's disease, or that it results from it. It may be unrelated. Further experiments are required to fully characterize the relationship between the component and the illness.

9. A: As stated in the text, the size of each circle is proportional to the number of recoveries.

10. J: The graph shows that the largest number of circles, and the largest circles as well, are at this depth. Since the size of the circles is proportional to the number of fish recovered, the greatest numbers of these fish were at these depths.

11. C: 2011 fish were recovered out of 34,000 released. The percentage is given by
$$P = 100 \times \frac{2,011}{34,000} = 6\%$$
.

12. G: The median age at each depth is shown by the X symbols on the plot. For this depth, the symbol lines up approximately with the mark corresponding to 5 years on the upper axis of the graph.

13. D: Although not specifically described in the text, all of the reasons stated may occur, reducing the recovery of tagged fish. The conclusions of the study must assume that the fraction of fish recovered (sample) are representative of the population as a whole.

14. J: The chart describes the age of the fish, but does not provide any information concerning their size.

15. B: The median age of the populations recovered at each depth is shown by the X symbol on the plot, and corresponds to progressively older fish at greater depths. Although some of the other statements are true, they are not supported by the data in the figure.

16. H: The right-most symbol on the plot shows that some 20-year old fish were recovered at depths of 501-700 meters. No older fish were recovered in this study.

17. D: The table shows that the lambda particle has a mass of over 1115 MeV

18. H: Protons and other nucleons are baryons, which are made of quarks. The other choices are all leptons, which are not.

19. D: To satisfy the law of conservation of charge, the net charge of all the particles produced in a decay must equal that of the original particle. Note that while conservation of mass applies to the decay, it does not pertain to charge.

20. J: The most massive particles of neutral charge are the Xi particles, with a mass of 1314.9 MeV.

21. A: The lambda particle has no charge. The proton has a charge of +1. To satisfy the law of conservation of charge, the other particle must have a charge of -1. The negative pion is the only choice that satisfies that condition.

22. H: The mass of the muon is 105.65 MeV. That of the positron is 0.65 MeV. To satisfy the law of conservation of mass, the mass of the positron plus that of the other resulting particles cannot add up to more than 105.65 MeV. Among the choices given, only the neutrino is small enough to satisfy that condition.

23. A: To satisfy the law of conservation of mass, the mass difference between the original particle and its decay products is released as knetic energy. Since the omega particle has a mass of 1672.45 MeV, and the kaon and lambda particles have masses of 493.68 and 1115.68 MeV, respectively, the difference is 63.09 MeV.

24. G: One MeV is equivalent to 1.783×10^{-30} kilogram, so that $60kg = \dfrac{60}{1.783 \times 10^{-30}}$ MeV = 33.65×10^{30} MeV.

25. C: Of the sites listed, the phi value for site MD, 2.73 phi, is the largest value. The text explains how phi varies inversely with particle size, so these are the smallest particles.

26. J: According to the definition of phi supplied in the text, the range 1.0 to 4.0 phi units corresponds to particle sizes in the range 0.06 to 0.5 mm.

27. A: At all of the sites except site ND, the particle size distributions are tightly centered around a well-defined modal value. At site ND, the distribution is spread out over a broader range, and there is no well-defined central value.

28. J: Each unit of added phi value in the negative direction corresponds to a doubling of the particle size, so that -1 corresponds to 2mm, -2 to 4 mm, and -3 to 8 mm.

29. A: The curves represent the distance traveled, and they approximate a straight line. The slope of the line represents the speed of travel. Although the curve in part (b) has a negative slope, the absolute value of that slope will be a positive value, representing speed of transport towards the west.

30. G: The steepest slopes correspond to the greatest values of mab, or meters above bottom. These are the shallowest waters.

31. B: The steepest slopes correspond to the greatest values of mab, or meters above bottom. These are the shallowest waters. Although the slopes are negative in this plot, it is the magnitude of the slope that indicates the speed of transport. Here, the negative value simply indicates that the sediments drift toward the west, not the east.

32. G: The upper graph shows transport toward the north. The lower graph shows transport toward the west. If these two are combined, overall transport will be toward the NW.

33. C: The efficiency curve in part B of the figure has a clear maximum value at a wind velocity of 10 m/s.

34. J: The power curve in part A of the figure increases with increasing wind velocity, until a plateau is reached at 15 m/s and above.

35. B: The text explains that for wind velocities above 15 m/s, the rotor blades are trimmed to protect the equipment. Above 25 m/s, the turbine must be shut down.

36. H: Power increases with the cube of wind velocity. This is an exponential function.

37. D: The power increases with the cube, or third power, of wind velocity, v. If the wind velocity is doubled, the power output will be proportional to the third power of the new wind velocity v'. But if v' = 2v, then
$$v'^3 = (2v)^3 = 8v^3$$
and the new power output is 8 times greater than the original output, or 1600 kW.

38. G: See question 37. Since this generator operates at 50% efficiency, only half of the theoretical power is available.

39. C: The longest bars in the histogram correspond to the middle frequencies, from about 300 to 2000 Hz.

40. J: The text explains that winds originate from differential warming of the earth's surface by the sun. It is this energy that is captured by a wind turbine.

Practice Test #2

Practice Questions

English

Questions 1-30 pertain to the following passage:

The Washingtons (1) had went on many good vacations, but (2) there all-time favorite one was when they visited (3) Mr. Washington's cousin Lucy at her home by Lake Tahoe.

Mr. and Mrs. Washington and their kids Arlo and Ella (4) piled onto the family car surrounded by clothes and (5) fishing equipments and presents for (6) Lucy and Lucys family, (7) rolled down their windows, and drove away. Penny the dog came (8) to and sat on the seat (9) next from Ella. Ella was (10) an avid painter, so they brought her backpack with all her paints and brushes so she could do paintings of the lake.

They (11) had been drive for about two hours when they decided to stop for lunch. Mrs. Washington (12) pulls the car of the highway and stopped by a shady tree. (13) As they getting out, Mr. Washington grabbed a pen to use for (14) filing in a crossword puzzle. The pen leaked and he got a stripe of blue ink on his hand, which he absentmindedly wiped on his white t-shirt. (15) Everybody get out of the car, put down blankets to sit on, and got out the sandwiches and drinks. Penny (16) drank all her food up and lay down on the blanket for a nap in the sun. Arlo and Ella (17) then decide to climb the tree. Ella kept her backpack on when she climbed.

Under the tree, Mr. Washington was tired and lay down next to Penny who (18) was dreaming and kick in her sleep. He pulled his hat over his eyes and (19) fell quick asleep. Mrs. Washington enjoyed the quiet and (20) read her book until she ate her sandwich. Suddenly, a wasp flew close to her and (21) startles her, and she dropped her sandwich on Mr. Washington; mustard from her sandwich spilled on his shirt. She gasped, which (22) woken up Penny, who jumped into the tomato salad and fell against Mr. Washington with her paws covered in tomato juice. Ella was getting crackers (23) in of her backpack and looked down and laughed so hard at what (24) she seen that she dropped her backpack with the paints in it. The green paint did not have (25) it's lid screwed on tightly and fell on Mr. Washington next to the red, yellow, and blue marks, leaving a green mark.

Mr. Washington was (26) wild awake now and looking with (27) surprised at his shirt. Everyone else was laughing. Arlo then got sad that he (28) hadn't help color his dad's shirt, so he found a (29) plumb in the cooler and looked at his dad questioningly. Mr. Washington sighed and nodded with (30) resignment. Arlo bit the fruit and rubbed it on his dad's shirt.

When they got to Lake Tahoe, Lucy's four-year-old daughter came to the door and squealed when she saw them. She yelled to her mom, "Mom, Uncle Rainbow is here!" That's what she's called him ever since.

1. A. no change
   B. has went
   C. gone
   D. had gone

2. F. no change
   G. they're
   H. their
   J. theyre

3. A. no change
   B. Mr. Washingtons'
   C. Mr. Washington
   D. Mr. Washington'

4. F. no change
   G. piled into the family car
   H. piled atop the family car
   J. piling into the family car

5. A. no change
   B. fishing equipment
   C. fishing equip
   D. equipments for fishing

6. F. no change
   G. Lucy and Lucys' family
   H. Lucy and Lucy's family
   J. Lucy and their family

7. A. no change
   B. rolled down his window
   C. rolled down their window
   D. rolled down windows

8. F. no change
   G. two
   H. too
   J. though

9. A. no change
   B. next by Ella
   C. next Ella
   D. next to Ella

10. F. no change
     G. a avid painter
     H. her avid painter
     J. avidly a painter

11. A. no change
    B. had drive
    C. had drived
    D. had been driving

12. F. no change
    G. pulled the car off the highway
    H. pulled the car of the highway
    J. pulls the car off the highway

13. A. no change
    B. As they were getting out
    C. As they get out
    D. As getting out

14. F. no change
    G. filing a crossword puzzle
    H. filling in a crossword puzzle
    J. filing a crossword puzzle

15. A. no change
    B. Everybody gets out of the car
    C. Everybody out of the car
    D. Everybody got out of the car

16. F. no change
    G. drank her food
    H. ate all her food
    J. drank some of her food

17. A. no change
    B. decide
    C. all decided
    D. then decided

18. F. no change
    G. was dreaming and kicking
    H. dreamt and kick
    J. was dreaming of kicking

19. A. no change
    B. fell quickly
    C. quick fell
    D. fall quickly

20. F. no change
    G. read her book as she ate
    H. read her book, ate
    J. read her book and she ate

21. A. no change
    B. startle
    C. startled
    D. was startling

22. F. no change
    G. woke up
    H. awokened
    J. awakes

23. A. no change
    B. in to
    C. from of
    D. out of

24. F. no change
    G. she sees
    H. she saw
    J. she seeing

25. A. no change
    B. its lid
    C. its' lid
    D. it lid

26. F. no change
    G. wide awake
    H. wildly awake
    J. widely awake

27. A. no change
    B. surprising
    C. surprise
    D. stupor

28. F. no change
    G. had helped
    H. hadn't helped
    J. helped

29. A. no change
    B. plum
    C. plump
    D. plumm

30. F. no change
   G. resigned
   H. resigning
   J. resignation

Questions 31-60 pertain to the following passage:

Danny and Carla (31) <u>were being married</u> for two years. For (32) <u>there</u> honeymoon, they (33) <u>hadgone</u> to the Grand Cayman Island for a nice, relaxing vacation at a luxury beach resort. But their honeymoon turned out to be anything but relaxing.

When (34) <u>they were arriving</u> at the airport, they hailed a taxi. The taxi driver strapped the suitcases to the top of the car and sped off towards the resort. Along the way, the taxi driver swerved (35) <u>to avoid hit</u> a cat on the road. This caused (36) <u>Carla'</u> suitcase to fly off the car and crash in the road. Her clothes, shoes, and personal items (37) <u>had flown</u> everywhere. She yelled (38) <u>anger</u> at the driver to stop immediately. Danny and Carla rushed out of the cab to gather her belongings. Once they collected everything they (39) <u>can find</u>, they started again for the resort. When they finally arrived, the driver charged them for the time spent collecting the things on the road. Irate, Danny made sure not to tip him.

Exhausted, Danny and Carla checked into their room. When they got to the room, they noticed they did not have a beachfront view as they (40) <u>had been promised</u>. They were also in a smoking room even though they had requested a non-smoking room. Danny asked to switch rooms, but the concierge (41) <u>apollageticaly</u> replied that they were booked for the rest of the week. "(42) <u>Its</u> a popular week for tourists, sir," she replied. Nothing (43) <u>could be done</u>. Danny, (44) <u>that</u> was trying to stay positive, told Carla not to worry. As long as they kept the windows open, the smell of cigarettes would not be (45) <u>to</u> much of a bother.

The next day, they (46) <u>waked up</u> early to fish and then go to the beach. They walked (47) <u>at the beach</u> and found a small table, two chairs, and a large umbrella. Then, they rented a boat to fish. Carla caught only one fish, but Danny (48) <u>catched several fishes</u>. When they got back, they took a nap on the beach. They finally felt peaceful. A few minutes later, a large family with six kids took a space right next to them. The kids were loud. Some of the kids were arguing, while some ran around squealing in delight. Danny and Carla were unable to sleep, so Danny suggested they (49) <u>went for a walk</u> together. Not paying attention to where they were walking, Carla suddenly jumped up and screamed in agony. She had stepped on a jellyfish and (50) <u>had got</u> stung. She was in pain and couldn't walk, so Danny (51) <u>had carried</u> her all the way back to the room.

Back (52) <u>into the room</u>, Danny (53) <u>realizing they had left</u> their things at the beach. Just as he was about to get them, it started to (54) <u>poor</u>. Danny hoped the umbrella would keep their things dry, but the wind (55) <u>was knocked</u> the umbrella over and everything (56) <u>were soaked</u>. Their books, phones, and wallet (57) <u>was ruinned</u>. To make matters worse, the rain didn't stop. Two days (58) <u>went by</u>. They had to stay in their smelly room, Carla was still in pain, and Danny was in a bad mood. Needless to say, they (59) <u>gone</u> home early. They thought they might be able to get their money back from the travel agent, but that was also (60) <u>unsuccessfull</u>.

- 76 -

31. A. no change
    B. were been married
    C. have been married
    D. were married

32. F. no change
    G. their
    H. they're
    J. theyre

33. A. no change
    B. had went
    C. gone
    D. went

34. F. no change
    G. they were arrived
    H. they arrived
    J. they are arriving

35. A. no change
    B. to avoid hitting
    C. to avoid hiting
    D. to avoid hitted

36. F. no change
    G. Carlas
    H. Carlas'
    J. Carla's

37. A. no change
    B. flyed
    C. flew
    D. flown

38. F. no change
    G. in an angry way
    H. angrily
    J. angrier

39. A. no change
    B. can found
    C. could find
    D. could found

40. F. no change
    G. were being promised
    H. are promised
    J. promised

41. A. no change
    B. apologetically
    C. apollogetically
    D. apollagetically

42. F. no change
    G. It
    H. It's
    J. It was

43. A. no change
    B. could have done
    C. could done
    D. could been done

44. F. no change
    G. whose
    H. who
    J. which

45. A. no change
    B. two
    C. too
    D. soo

46. F. no change
    G. woken up
    H. woked up
    J. woke up

47. A. no change
    B. to the beach
    C. in the beach
    D. for the beach

48. F. no change
    G. catched several fish
    H. caught several fish
    J. caught several fishes

49. A. no change
    B. go for a walk
    C. going for a walk
    D. had gone for a walk

50. F. no change
    G. had get
    H. got
    J. gotten

51. A. no change
    B. was carried
    C. was carrying
    D. carried

52. F. no change
    G. in the room
    H. for the room
    J. on the room

53. A. no change
    B. had realized they had left
    C. realized they had left
    D. realizing they were leaving

54. F. no change
    G. pour
    H. porre
    J. pore

55. A. no change
    B. was knock
    C. knocking
    D. had knocked

56. F. no change
    G. was soaked
    H. were soaking
    J. was soak

57. A. no change
    B. was ruined
    C. were ruined
    D. were ruinned

58. F. no change
    G. gone by
    H. went
    J. gone past

59. A. no change
    B. had gone
    C. went
    D. will be going

60. F. no change
    G. unsuccessful
    H. unsucesful
    J. unsuccesful

Questions 61-75 pertain to the following passage:

(61)<u>People have always color fabrics with dyes</u>. (62)<u>People use to get dyes</u> (63)<u>from those plants they found around them</u>. Different regions had different plants (64)<u>and variously techniques for dyeing</u>. In colonial days, (65)<u>dyeing in Europe were craft skills</u> (66)<u>gained by lengthy apprenticeship</u>. The men who practiced these arts knew biology and chemistry to understand their (67)<u>materials which came from plants, minerals, and animals</u>. (68)<u>Manufacturing natural dyes required much skill</u>, especially for complicated dyes like indigo.

(69)<u>Indigo is maybe the oldest natural dye</u>. The indigo plant stands three feet tall and (70)<u>the dye comprises only 1/2% of the plant's weight</u>. (71)<u>Lots of species of three different plant families</u>, widely scattered over the world, contain enough dye to be worth cultivating, (72)<u>but tropical were especially prized</u> for the quality of color they produced. (73)<u>From India and Africa, for example, came the best indigo.</u>

(74)<u>Native Americans were for long expert dyers before the arrival of Europeans</u>. The American colonists (75)<u>used their dyes and methods they brought from Europe</u>, but over time they turned to dyes made from native plants, as well, to supplement those imported from Europe. During the early 19th century, dyeing became a specialized skill and sometimes moved outside the home to a special site. While most women continued to dye many fabrics at home, large pieces of cloth for domestic use and fabrics needed for manufacturing began to be dyed by professionals.

61. A. No change
    B. People always did color fabrics with dyes.
    C. People have always colored fabrics with dyes.
    D. People have always colored, fabrics with dyes.

62. F. No change
    G. People got dyes
    H. People use to got dyes
    J. People used to get dyes

63. A. No change
    B. from the plants they found around them
    C. from some plants they found around them
    D. from the plants, they found around them

64. F. No change
    G. and often techniques for dyeing
    H. and different techniques for dying
    J. and different techniques for dyeing

65. A. No change
    B. dyeing in Europe were skills
    C. dyeing in Europe were crafts
    D. dyeing in Europe was a craft skill

66. F. No change
    G. gained by longer apprenticeship
    H. gaining a long apprenticeship
    J. for which one gained a long apprenticeship

67. A. No change
    B. materials, which came from plants, minerals, and animals
    C. materials; which came from plants, minerals, and animals
    D. materials: which came from plants, minerals, and animals

68. F. No change
    G. Manufacturing natural dyes required many skill
    H. Manufacturing natural dyes required more skill
    J. Manufacturing natural dyes was in need of much skill

69. A. No change
    B. Maybe indigo is the oldest natural dye.
    C. Indigo maybe is the oldest natural dye.
    D. Indigo is probably the oldest natural dye.

70. F. No change
    G. the dye composes only 1/2% of the plant's weight.
    H. the dye consists of only 1/2% of the plant's weight.
    J. the dye is comprising of only 1/2% of the plant's weight.

71. A. No change
    B. Many species of three different plant families
    C. Lots of species in three different plant families
    D. Lots of different plant families

72. F. No change
    G. but tropical varieties were especially prized
    H. but tropical kind were especially prized
    J. but, tropical ones were especially prized

73. A. No change
    B. From India and Africa, for example, the best indigo came.
    C. The best indigo came from India and Africa, for example.
    D. For example, came the best indigo from India and Africa.

74. F. No change
    G. Native Americans were long expert dyers before the arrival of Europeans.
    H. Native Americans for long were expert dyers before the arrival of Europeans.
    J. Native Americans were expert dyers long before the arrival of Europeans.

75. A. No change
    B. used their dyes and methods that they brought from Europe
    C. used the dyes and methods they brought from Europe
    D. used they're dyes and methods from Europe

Mathematics

1. Jamie had $6.50 in his wallet when he left home. He spent $4.25 on drinks, and $2.00 on a magazine. Later, his friend repaid him $2.50, which he had borrowed the previous day. How much money does Jamie have in his wallet?
    A. $12.25
    B. $14.25
    C. $3.25
    D. $2.75
    E. $1.75

Question 2 is based on the following table:

English-Metric Equivalents	
1 meter	1.094 yards
2.54 centimeters	1 inch
1 kilogram	2.205 pounds
1 liter	1.06 quarts

2. A sailboat is 19 meters long. What is its length in inches?
    F. 254 inches
    G. 1094 inches
    H. 4826 inches
    J. 748 inches
    K. 21 inches

3. Mrs. Patterson's classroom has sixteen empty chairs. All of the chairs are occupied when every student is present. If 2/5 of the students are absent, how many students make up her entire class?
    A. 16 students
    B. 32 students
    C. 24 students
    D. 40 students
    E. 36 students

4. Rachel spent $24.15 on vegetables. She bought 2 lbs of onions, 3 lbs of carrots, and 1 ½ lbs of mushrooms. If the onions cost $3.69 per lb, and the carrots cost $ 4.29 per lb, what is the price per lb of mushrooms?

    F. $2.60
    G. $2.25
    H. $2.80
    J. $3.10
    K. $2.75

Question 5 is based on the following figure:

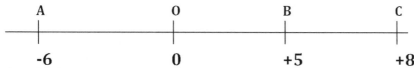

5. In the figure, A, B, and C are points on the number line, where O is the origin. What is the ratio of the distance BC to distance AB?

    A. 3:5
    B. 8:5
    C. 8:11
    D. 3:11
    E. 8:6

6. A long distance runner does a first lap around a track in exactly 50 seconds. As she tires, each subsequent lap takes 20% longer than the previous one. How long does she take to run 3 laps?

    F. 180 seconds
    G. 182 seconds
    H. 160 seconds
    J. 72 seconds
    K. 150 seconds

7. In an election in Kimball County, Candidate A obtained 36,800 votes. His opponent, Candidate B, obtained 32,100 votes. 2,100 votes went to write-in candidates. What percentage of the vote went to Candidate A?

    A. 51.8%
    B. 53.4%
    C. 45.2%
    D. 46.8%
    E. 56.2%

8.

y	-4	31	4	68	12
x	-2	3	0	4	2

Which of the following equations satisfies the five sets of numbers shown in the above table?

F. $y = 2x^2 + 7$
G. $y = x^3 + 4$
H. $y = 2x$
J. $y = 3x + 1$
K. $y = 6x$

9. In a rectangular xy coordinate system, what is the intersection of two lines formed by the equations $y = 2x + 3$ and $y = x - 5$?

A. (5, 3)
B. (8, 13)
C. (-4, 13)
D. (-8, -13)
E. (2, -7)

Question 10 is based on the following figure:

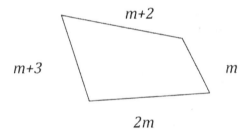

10. The figure shows an irregular quadrilateral, and the lengths of its individual sides. Which of the following equations best represents the perimeter of the quadrilateral?

F. $m^4 + 5$
G. $2m^4 + 5$
H. $4m + 5$
J. $5m + 5$
K. $4m^2 + 5$

Questions 11 – 13 are based on the following table, which describes the closing prices of a number of stocks traded on the New York Stock Exchange:

Stock	Price per Share	Shares Traded
Microsoft	$45.14	89,440,000
Oracle	$19.11	12,415,000
Apple Computer	$16.90	17,953,000
Cisco Systems	$3.50	73,019,000
Garmin	$29.30	53,225,000

11. David bought 200 shares of Oracle stock yesterday, and sold it today. His profit was $22.00. At what price did he buy the stock yesterday?
   A. $18.89
   B. $19.00
   C. $19.06
   D. $18.96
   E. $18.80

12. A function *f(x)* is defined by $f(x) = 2x^2 + 7$. What is the value of $2f(x) - 3$?
   F. $4x^2 + 11$
   G. $4x^4 + 11$
   H. $x^2 + 11$
   J. $4x^2 + 14$
   K. $2x^2 + 14$

13. John buys 100 shares of stock at $100 per share. The price goes up by 10%, and he sells 50 shares. Then, prices drop by 10%, and he sells his remaining 50 shares. How much did he get for the last 50 shares?
   A. $5000
   B. $5500
   C. $4900
   D. $5050
   E. $4950

14. The two shortest sides of a right triangle are 6 and 8 units long, respectively. What is the length of the perimeter?
   F. 10 units
   G. 18 units
   H. 24 units
   J. 14 units
   K. 36 units

Question 15 is based on the following diagram:

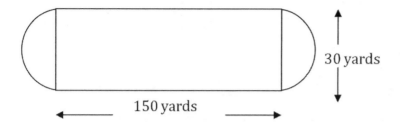

30 yards

150 yards

15. The diagram shows the outline of a racetrack for skaters, which consists of two long, straight sections, and two semi-circular turns. Given the dimensions shown, which of the following most closely measures the perimeter of the entire track?
   A. 300 yards
   B. 180 yards
   C. 360 yards
   D. 395 yards
   E. 425 yards

16. Elijah drove 45 miles to his job in an hour and ten minutes in the morning. On the way home, however, traffic was much heavier, and the same trip took an hour and a half. What was his average speed in miles per hour for the round trip?
   F. 30 mph
   G. 45 mph
   H. 33 ¾ mph
   J. 32 ½ mph
   K. 35 mph

17. What is the area of an isosceles triangle inscribed in a circle of radius r, if the base of the triangle is the diameter of the circle?
   A. r^2
   B. $2r^2$
   C. πr^2
   D. $2\pi r$
   E. $2\pi + 1$

18. Lauren had $80 in her savings account. When she received her paycheck, she made a deposit, which brought the balance up to $120. By what percentage did the total amount in her account increase as a result of this deposit?
   F. 50%
   G. 40%
   H. 35%
   J. 80%
   K. 120%

19. A regular deck of cards has 52 cards. What is the probability of drawing three aces in a row?
    A. 1 in 52
    B. 1 in 156
    C. 1 in 2000
    D. 1 in 5525
    E. 1 in 132600

20. Which of the following is a solution to the inequality $4x - 12 < 4$?
    F. 7
    G. 6
    H. 5
    J. 4
    K. 3

21. If a = -6 and b = 7, then $4a(3b + 5) + 2b$ = ?
    A. 638
    B. 624
    C. 610
    D. -610
    E. -638

22. Mark is driving to Phoenix from a city located 210 miles north. He drives the first ten miles in 12 minutes. If he continues at the same rate, how long will it take him to reach his destination?
    F. 3 hours 15 minutes
    G. 4 hours 12 minutes
    H. 3 hours 45 minutes
    J. 4 hours 20 minutes
    K. 3 hours 52 minutes

23. An airplane leaves Atlanta at 2 PM, and flies north at 250 miles per hour. A second airplane leaves Atlanta 30 minutes later, and flies north at 280 miles per hour. At what time will the second airplane overtake the first?
    A. 6:00 PM
    B. 6:20 PM
    C. 6:40 PM
    D. 6:50 PM
    E. 7:10 PM

Question 24 is based on the following diagram:

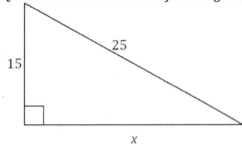

24. Find the length of the side labeled x. The triangle represented in the figure is a right triangle, as shown.
    F. 18
    G. 20
    H. 22
    J. 24
    K. 25

25. A motorcycle manufacturer offers 3 different models, each available in 6 different colors. How many different combinations of model and color are available?
    A. 9
    B. 6
    C. 12
    D. 18
    E. 24

26. If $x + y > 0$ when $x > y$, which of the following cannot be true?
    F. $x = 3$ and $y = 0$
    G. $x = 6$ and $y = -1$
    H. $x = -3$ and $y = 0$
    J. $x = -4$ and $y = -3$
    K. $x = 3$ and $y = -3$

27. Which of the following expressions is equivalent to $x^3 x^5$?
    A. $2x^8$
    B. x^{15}
    C. x^2
    D. x^8
    E. $2x^{15}$

28. If $\dfrac{12}{x} = \dfrac{30}{6}$, what is the value of x?
    F. 3.6
    G. 2.4
    H. 3.0
    J. 2.0
    K. 2.75

29. Which of the following could be a graph of the function $y = \dfrac{1}{x}$?

A.

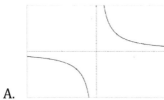

B.

C.

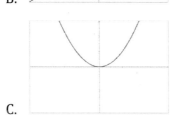

D.

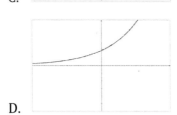

E.

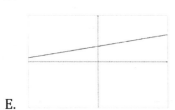

Question 30 is based on the following figure:

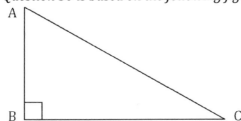

30. ΔABC is a right triangle, and ∠ACB = 30°. What is the measure of ∠BAC?
    F. 40°
    G. 50°
    H. 60°
    J. 45°
    K. 70°

Question 31 is based on the following table:

Hours	1	2	3
Cost	$3.60	$7.20	$10.80

31. The table shows the cost of renting a bicycle for 1, 2, or 3 hours. Which of the following equations best represents the data, if C represents the cost and h represents the time of the rental?
    A. $C = 3.60h$
    B. $C = h + 3.60$
    C. $C = 3.60h + 10.80$
    D. $C = 10.80/h$
    E. $C = 3.60 + 7.20h$

Question 32 is based on the following figure:

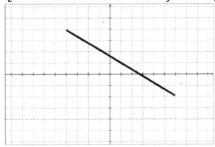

32. Which of the following are complementary angles?
    F. 71° and 19°
    G. 18° and 18°
    H. 90° and 90°
    J. 90° and 45°
    K. 15° and 30°

33. Which of the following statements is true?
   A. Perpendicular lines have opposite slopes
   B. Perpendicular lines have the same slopes
   C. Perpendicular lines have reciprocal slopes
   D. Perpendicular lines have opposite reciprocal slopes
   E. Perpendicular lines have slopes that are unrelated

34. There are 64 squares on a checkerboard. Bobby puts one penny on the first square, two on the second square, four on the third, eight on the fourth, and continues to double the number of coins at each square until he has covered all 64 squares. How many coins must he place upon the last square?
   F. 2^{64}
   G. $2^{64} - 1$
   H. 2^{63}
   J. $2^{63} + 1$
   K. $2^{64} - 2$

35. Carrie wants to decorate her party with bundles of balloons, containing three balloons each. Balloons are available in 4 different colors. There must be three different colors in each bundle. How many different kinds of bundles can she make?
   A. 18
   B. 12
   C. 4
   D. 6
   E. 10

Question 36 is based on the following figure:

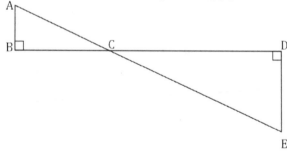

36. In the figure above, segment BC is 4 units long, segment CD is 8 units long, and segment DE is 6 units long. What is the length of segment AC?
   F. 7 units
   G. 5 units
   H. 3 units
   J. 2.5 units
   K. 4 units

37. If p and n are positive, consecutive integers such that $p > n$, and $p+n=15$, what is the value of n?

 A. 5
 B. 6
 C. 7
 D. 8
 E. 9

38. In a game of chance, 3 dice are cast simultaneously. What is the probability that all three will land with a 6 showing?

 F. 1 in 6
 G. 1 in 18
 H. 1 in 216
 J. 1 in 30
 K. 1 in 36

39. Rafael has a business selling computers. He buys computers from the manufacturer for $450 each, and sells them for $800. Each month, he must also pay fixed costs of $3000 for rent and utilities at his store. If he sells n computers in a month, which of the following equations can be used to calculate his profit?

 A. $P = n(800 - 450)$
 B. $P = n(800 - 450 - 3000)$
 C. $P = 3000n(800 - 450)$
 D. $P = n(800 - 450) - 3000$
 E. $P = n(800 - 450) + 3000$

40. Arrange the following numbers in order, from least to greatest: 2^3, 4^2, 6^0, 9, and 10^1.

 F. 2^3, 4^2, 6^0, 9, 10^1
 G. 6^0, 9, 10^1, 2^3, 4^2
 H. 10^1, 2^3, 6^0, 9, 4^2
 J. 6^0, 2^3, 9, 10^1, 4^2
 K. 9, 6^0, 10^1, 4^2, 2^3

41. Which of the following expressions represents the ratio of the area of a circle to its circumference?

 A. πr^2
 B. $\dfrac{\pi r^2}{2\pi}$
 C. $\dfrac{2\pi r}{r^2}$
 D. $2\pi r^{1/2}$
 E. $\dfrac{r}{2}$

- 92 -

Questions 42-43 are based on the following chart:

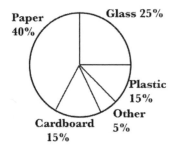

42. The Charleston Recycling Company collects 50,000 tons of recyclable materials every month. The chart shows the kinds of materials that are collected by the company's five trucks. What is the second most common material that is recycled?
  F. Cardboard
  G. Glass
  H. Paper
  J. Plastic
  K. Other

43. Approximately how much paper is recycled every month?
  A. 40,000 tons
  B. 50,000 tons
  C. 60,000 tons
  D. 15,000 tons
  E. 20,000 tons

44. Dorothy is half of her sister's age. In 20 years, she will be three-fourths of her sister's age. How old is she?
  F. 10 years
  G. 15 years
  H. 20 years
  J. 25 years
  K. 30 years

45. If x and y are positive integers, which of the following expressions is equivalent to $(xy)^{7y} - (xy)^y$?
  A. $(xy)^{6y}$
  B. $(xy)^{7y-1}$
  C. $(xy)^y[(xy)^7 - 1]$
  D. $(xy)^y[(xy)^{6y} - 1]$
  E. $(xy)^{7y}$

Question 46 is based on the following diagram:

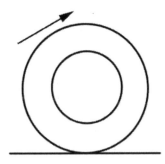

46. A tire on a car rotates at 500 RPM (revolutions per minute) when the car is traveling at 50 km/hr (kilometers per hour). What is the circumference of the tire, in meters?

F. $\dfrac{50,000}{2\pi}$ meters

G. $\dfrac{50,000}{60 \times 2\pi}$ meters

H. $\dfrac{50,000}{500 \times 2\pi}$ meters

J. $\dfrac{50,000}{60}$ meters

K. $\dfrac{10}{6}$ meters

47. A combination lock uses a 3-digit code. Each digit can be any one of the ten available integers 0-9. How many different combinations are possible?

A. 9
B. 1000
C. 30
D. 81
E. 100

48. Which of the following expressions is equivalent to $(a + b)(a - b)$?

F. $a^2 - b^2$
G. $(a + b)^2$
H. $(a - b)^2$
J. $ab(a - b)$
K. $ab(a + b)$

Questions 49 and 50 are based on the following table:

Kyle bats third in the batting order for the Badgers baseball team. The table below shows the number of hits that Kyle had in each of 7 consecutive games played during one week in July.

Day of Week	Number of Hits
Monday	1
Tuesday	2
Wednesday	3
Thursday	1
Friday	1
Saturday	4
Sunday	2

49. What is the mode of the numbers in the distribution shown in the table?
  A. 1
  B. 2
  C. 3
  D. 4
  E. 7

50. What is the mean of the numbers in the distribution shown in the table?
  F. 1
  G. 2
  H. 3
  J. 4
  K. 7

51. Forty students in a class take a test that is graded on a scale of 1 to 10. The histogram in the figure shows the grade distribution, with the *x*-axis representing the grades, and the *y*-axis representing the number of students who obtain each grade. If the mean, median, and modal values are represented by *n*, *p*, and *q*, respectively, which of the following is true?

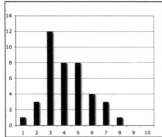

  A. $n > p > q$
  B. $n > q > p$
  C. $q > p > n$
  D. $p > q > n$
  E. $q > n > p$

52. Referring again to the figure for the previous question, if the top 10% of students are to receive a grade of A, what is the minimum test score required to get an A?

F. 10
G. 9
H. 8
J. 7
K. 6

53.

Lemons	35%
Sugar	20%
Cups	25%
Stand improvements	5%
Profits	15%

Herbert plans to use the earnings from his lemonade stand according to the table above, for the first month of operations. If he buys $70 worth of lemons, how much profit does he take home?

A. $15
B. $20
C. $30
D. $35.50
E. $40

54. If $10x + 2 = 7$, what is the value of $2x$?

F. 0.5
G. -0.5
H. 1
J. 5
K. 10

55. A number N is multiplied by 3. The result is the same as when N is divided by 3. What is the value of N?

A. 1
B. 0
C. -1
D. 3
E. -3

56. The letter H exhibits symmetry with respect to a horizontal axis, as shown in the figure, as everything below the dashed line is a mirror image of everything above it. Which of the following letters does NOT exhibit horizontal symmetry?

F. C
G. D
H. E
J. I
K. Z

57. A teacher has 3 hours to grade all of the papers submitted by the 35 students in her class. She gets through the first 5 papers in 30 minutes. How much faster does she have to work to grade the remaining papers in the allotted time?
    A. 10%
    B. 15%
    C. 20%
    D. 25%
    E. 30%

58. A sailor judges the distance to a lighthouse by holding a ruler at arm's length, and then measuring the apparent height of the lighthouse. He knows that the lighthouse is actually 60 feet tall. If it appears to be 3 inches tall when the ruler is held 2 feet from his eye, how far away is it?

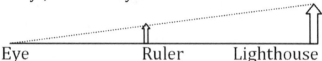

Eye   Ruler   Lighthouse
    F. 60 feet
    G. 120 feet
    H. 240 feet
    J. 480 feet
    K. 960 feet

59. What is the area of a square inscribed within a circle of radius r?
    A. r^2
    B. $2r^2$
    C. $2r^3$
    D. $2\pi r$
    E. $4r^2$

60. The sides of a triangle are equal to integral numbers of units. Two sides are 4 and 6 units long, respectively. What is the minimum value for the triangle's perimeter?
    F. 10 units
    G. 11 units
    H. 12 units
    J. 13 units
    K. 9 units

Reading

Questions 1-10 pertain to the following passage:

Garth

The next morning she realized that she had slept. This surprised her – so long had sleep been denied her! She opened her eyes and saw the sun at the window. And then, beside it in the window, the deformed visage of Garth. Quickly, she shut her eyes again, feigning sleep. But he was not fooled. Presently she heard his voice, soft and kind: "Don't be afraid. I'm your friend. I came to watch you sleep, is all. There now, I am behind the wall. You can open your eyes."

The voice seemed pained and plaintive. The Hungarian opened her eyes, saw the window empty. Steeling herself, she arose, went to it, and looked out. She saw the man below, cowering by the wall, looking grief-stricken and resigned. Making an effort to overcome her revulsion, she spoke to him as kindly as she could.

"Come," she said, but Garth, seeing her lips move, thought she was sending him away. He rose and began to lumber off, his eyes lowered and filled with despair.

"Come!" she cried again, but he continued to move off. Then, she swept from the cell, ran to him and took his arm. Feeling her touch, Garth trembled uncontrollably. Feeling that she drew him toward her, he lifted his supplicating eye and his whole face lit up with joy.

She drew him into the garden, where she sat upon a wall, and for a while they sat and contemplated one another. The more the Hungarian looked at Garth, the more deformities she discovered. The twisted spine, the lone eye, the huge torso over the tiny legs. She couldn't comprehend how a creature so awkwardly constructed could exist. And yet, from the air of sadness and gentleness that pervaded his figure, she began to reconcile herself to it.

"Did you call me back?" asked he.

"Yes," she replied, nodding. He recognized the gesture.

"Ah," he exclaimed. "Do you know that I am deaf?"

"Poor fellow," exclaimed the Hungarian, with an expression of pity.

"You'd think nothing more could be wrong with me," Garth put in, somewhat bitterly. But he was happier than he could remember having been.

1. Why was the girl surprised that she had slept?
    A. It was afternoon.
    B. She seldom slept.
    C. It had been a long time since she had had the chance to sleep.
    D. She hadn't intended to go to sleep.
    E. Garth looked so frightening that she thought he would keep her awake.

2. Why did she shut her eyes again when she saw Garth in the window?
    F. She wanted to sleep some more.
    G. The sun was so bright that it hurt her eyes.
    H. She didn't want to look at Garth.
    J. She wanted Garth to think she was still sleeping.
    K. She was trying to remember how she got there.

3. What two characteristics are contrasted in Garth?
    A. Ugliness and gentleness
    B. Fear and merriment
    C. Distress and madness
    D. Happiness and sadness
    E. Anger and fearfulness

4. During this passage, how do the girl's emotions toward Garth change?
    F. They go from fear to loathing.
    G. They go from anger to fear.
    H. They go from hatred to disdain.
    J. They go from fear to disdain.
    K. They go from revulsion to pity.

5. Why does the girl have to steel herself to approach the window and look out at Garth?
    A. She is groggy from sleep.
    B. She has not eaten for a long time.
    C. She is repelled by his appearance.
    D. She is blinded by the sun behind him.
    E. The window is open and it is cold.

6. How does Garth feel toward the girl when he first moves away from the window?
    F. He is curious about her.
    G. He is sad because she appears to reject him.
    H. He is angry at her for pretending to sleep.
    J. He pretends to be indifferent toward her.
    K. He expects her to scold him.

7. Why does Garth withdraw from the girl when she first speaks to him?
    A. He expects her to hurt him.
    B. He misunderstands her because he cannot hear.
    C. People are always mean to him.
    D. He thinks she wants to sleep some more.
    E. He doesn't want her to feel revulsion because of his appearance.

8. What is a synonym for the word *supplicating*?
   F. Castigating
   G. Menacing
   H. Repeating
   J. Begging
   K. Steeling

9. Why is it surprising that the girl takes Garth's arm?
   A. She is engaged to someone else.
   B. She has to reach through the window.
   C. He is deaf.
   D. She was very frightened of him initially.
   E. His clothes are dirty.

10. Which of the following adjectives might you use to describe the girl's personality?
    F. Determined
    G. Robust
    H. Manic
    J. Contemplative
    K. Sympathetic

Questions 11-20 pertain to the following passage:
New Zealand Inhabitants
The islands of New Zealand are among the most remote of all the Pacific islands. New Zealand is an archipelago, with two large islands and a number of smaller ones. Its climate is far cooler than the rest of Polynesia. Nevertheless, according to Maori legends, it was colonized in the early fifteenth century by a wave of Polynesian voyagers who traveled southward in their canoes and settled on NorthIsland. At this time, New Zealand was already known to the Polynesians, who had probably first landed there some 400 years earlier.

The Polynesian southward migration was limited by the availability of food. Traditional Polynesian tropical crops such as taro and yams will grow on NorthIsland, but the climate of South Island is too cold for them. Coconuts will not grow on either island. The first settlers were forced to rely on hunting and gathering, and, of course, fishing. Especially on South Island, most settlements remained close to the sea. At the time of the Polynesian influx, enormous flocks of moa birds had their rookeries on the island shores. These flightless birds were easy prey for the settlers, and within a few centuries had been hunted to extinction. Fish, shellfish and the roots of the fern were other important sources of food, but even these began to diminish in quantity as the human population increased. The Maori had few other sources of meat: dogs, smaller birds, and rats. Archaeological evidence shows that human flesh was also eaten, and that tribal warfare increased markedly after the moa disappeared.

By far the most important farmed crop in prehistoric New Zealand was the sweet potato. This tuber is hearty enough to grow throughout the islands, and could be stored to provide food during the winter months, when other food-gathering activities were difficult. The availability of the sweet potato made possible a significant increase in the human population. Maori tribes often lived in

- 100 -

encampments called *pa*, which were fortified with earthen embankments and usually located near the best sweet potato farmlands.

11. A definition for the word *archipelago* is
    A. A country
    B. A place in the southern hemisphere
    C. A group of islands
    D. A roosting place for birds
    E. A place with rainforests

12. This article is primarily about what?
    F. The geology of New Zealand
    G. New Zealand's early history
    H. New Zealand's prehistory
    J. Food sources used by New Zealand's first colonists.
    K. Polynesian emigration.

13. According to the passage, when was New Zealand first settled?
    A. In the fifteenth century
    B. Around the eleventh century
    C. Thousands of years ago
    D. On South Island
    E. By successive waves of people

14. Why did early settlements remain close to the sea?
    F. The people liked to swim.
    G. The people didn't want to get far from the boats they had come in.
    H. Taro and yams grow only close to the beaches.
    J. The seaside climate was milder.
    K. They were dependent upon sea creatures for their food.

15. Why do you suppose tribal warfare increased after the moa disappeared?
    A. Increased competition for food led the people to fight.
    B. Some groups blamed others for the moa's extinction.
    C. They had more time on their hands since they couldn't hunt the moa, so they fought.
    D. One group was trying to consolidate political control over the entire country.
    E. They wanted to appease the gods in the hope that the moa would return.

16. How did the colder weather of New Zealand make it difficult for the Polynesians to live there?
    F. The Polynesians weren't used to making warm clothes.
    G. Cold water fish are harder to catch.
    H. Some of them froze.
    J. Some of their traditional crops would not grow there.
    K. They had never seen snow.

17. What was a significant difference between the sweet potato and other crops known to the Polynesians?
    A. The sweet potato provided more protein.
    B. The sweet potato would grow on NorthIsland.
    C. The sweet potato could be stored during the winter.
    D. The sweet potato could be cultured near their encampments.
    E. The sweet potato did not need to be cultured near the shores.

18. Why was it important that sweet potatoes could be stored?
    F. They could be eaten in winter, when other foods were scarce.
    G. They could be traded for fish and other goods.
    H. They could be taken along by groups of warriors going to war.
    J. They tasted better after a few weeks of storage.
    K. They were kept in pa.

19. Why do you suppose the *pa* were usually located near sweet potato farmlands?
    A. So they could defend the best farmlands from their fortified camps.
    B. So they could have ready access to their most important source of food.
    C. So they could transport the potatoes easily into camp for storage.
    D. So they wouldn't have far to go from camp to work in the farmlands.
    E. All of the above are probably true.

20. Why might the shellfish populations have diminished as the human population increased?
    F. Too many people poisoned the waters.
    G. The shellfish didn't like people and migrated elsewhere.
    H. The people were hunting the natural predators of the shellfish to extinction.
    J. There were fewer nutrients left in the waters for the shellfish.
    K. The humans were eating the shellfish faster than they could replenish themselves through reproduction.

Questions 21-30 pertain to the following passage:

The Coins of Ancient Greece

We don't usually think of coins as works of art, and most of them really do not invite us to do so. The study of coins, their development and history, is termed *numismatics*. Numismatics is a topic of great interest to archeologists and anthropologists, but not usually from the perspective of visual delectation. The coin is intended, after all, to be a utilitarian object, not an artistic one. Many early Greek coins are aesthetically pleasing as well as utilitarian, however, and not simply because they are the earliest examples of the coin design. Rather, Greek civic individualism provides the reason. Every Greek political entity expressed its identity through its coinage.

The idea of stamping metal pellets of a standard weight with an identifying design had its origin on the IonianPeninsula around 600 B.C. Each of the Greek city-states produced its own coinage adorned with its particular symbols. The designs were changed frequently to commemorate battles, treaties, and other significant occasions. In addition to their primary use as a pragmatic means of facilitating commerce, Greek coins were clearly an expression of civic pride. The popularity of early coinage led to a constant demand for new designs, such that there arose a class of highly skilled artisans who took great pride in their work, so much so that they sometimes even signed it. As a result, Greek coins provide us not only with an invaluable source of historical knowledge, but also with a genuine expression of the evolving Greek sense of form, as well. These minuscule works reflect the development of Greek sculpture from the sixth to the second century B.C. as dependably as do larger works made of marble or other metals. And since they are stamped with the place and date of their production, they provide an historic record of artistic development that is remarkably dependable and complete.

21. What is the purpose of this passage?
    A. To attract new adherents to numismatics as a pastime.
    B. To show how ancient Greeks used coins in commerce.
    C. To teach the reader that money was invented in Greece.
    D. To describe ancient Greek coinage as an art form
    E. To show why coins are made of precious metals.

22. What is meant by the phrase "most of them do not invite us to do so", as used in the first sentence?
    F. Money is not usually included when sending an invitation.
    G. Most coins are not particularly attractive.
    H. Invitations are not generally engraved onto coins.
    J. Coins do not speak.
    K. It costs money to enter a museum.

23. What is a synonym for "delectation", as used in the third sentence?
    A. Savoring
    B. Choosing
    C. Deciding
    D. Refusing
    E. Consuming

24. What is meant by the term numismatics?
    F. The study of numbers
    G. Egyptian history
    H. Greek history
    J. The study of coins
    K. The study of commerce

25. According to the text, how do ancient Greek coins differ from most other coinage?
    A. Simply because they were the first coins.
    B. Each political entity made its own coins.
    C. They were made of precious metals.
    D. They had utilitarian uses.
    E. They were designed with extraordinary care.

26. How often were new coins designed in ancient Greece?
    F. Monthly
    G. Not very often.
    H. Whenever there was a significant occasion to commemorate.
    J. When the old ones wore out.
    K. In the year 600 B.C.

27. What is indicated by the fact that the artisans who designed the coins sometimes signed them?
    A. They took pride in their work.
    B. They were being held accountable for their work.
    C. The signature certified the value of the coin.
    D. The Greeks had developed writing.
    E. The coins that were signed were the most valuable.

28. What is meant by the term *pragmatic*, as used in the third sentence of the second paragraph?
    F. Valuable
    G. Monetary
    H. Useful
    J. Officious
    K. Practical

29. According to the passage, how are Greek coins similar to Greek sculpture?
    A. Some sculptures were made of metal.
    B. The coins were smaller.
    C. Shapes were stamped into the coins.
    D. Coin designs evolved along with the Greek sense of form.
    E. Both had pragmatic applications.

30. Why is it significant that new coin designs were required frequently?
    F. This indicates that there was a lot of commercial activity going on.
    G. This gave the designers a lot of practice.
    H. There were a lot of things to commemorate.
    J. The Greeks needed to find new sources of precious metals.
    K. The older coins could be recycled.

Questions 31-40 pertain to the following passage:

Annelids

The phylum Annelida, named for the Latin word *anellus*, meaning "ring", includes earthworms, leeches, and other similar organisms. In their typical form, these animals exhibit bilateral symmetry, a cylindrical cross section, and an elongate body divided externally into segments (*metameres*) by a series of rings (*annuli*). They are segmented internally as well, with most of the internal organs repeated in series in each segment. This organization is termed *metamerism*. Metameric segmentation is the distinguishing feature of this phylum, and provides it with a degree of evolutionary plasticity in that certain segments can be modified and specialized to perform specific functions. For example, in some species certain of the locomotor*parapodia*, or feet, may be modified for grasping, and some portions of the gut may evolve digestive specializations.

- 104 -

The gut is a straight, muscular tube that functions independently of the muscular activity in the body wall. The Annelida resemble the nematodes, another worm phylum, in possessing a fluid-filled internal cavity separating the gut from the body wall. In both phyla, this cavity is involved in locomotion. However, in the annelids this space is formed at a much later time during the development of the embryo, and presumably evolved much later as well. This fluid-filled internal space is called a true *coelum*.

The annelid excretory and circulatory systems are well developed, and some members of the phylum have evolved respiratory organs. The nervous system offers a particular example of metameric specialization. It is concentrated anteriorly into enlarged cerebral ganglia connected to a ventral nerve cord that extends posteriorly and is organized into repeating segmental ganglia.

This phylum includes members bearing adaptations required for aquatic (marine or freshwater) or terrestrial habitats. They may be free-living entities or exist as parasites. Among the best known are the earthworm *Lumbricus*, the water leech *Hirudo*, and the marine worm *Nereis*.

31. What is the purpose of this passage?
    A. To describe the annelid nervous system.
    B. To describe the annelid digestive system.
    C. To introduce distinctive features of annelid anatomy.
    D. To define metamerism.
    E. To tell readers about earthworms.

32. What is meant by the term *metamerism*?
    F. Segmentation of the anatomy
    G. A series of rings
    H. Bilateral symmetry
    J. Evolutionary plasticity
    K. Specialization

33. What is meant by the term *parapodia*?
    A. Specialization
    B. Grasping appendages
    C. Locomotion
    D. Metameres
    E. Feet

34. One evolutionary advantage of segmentation is that
    F. Segmented animals have many feet.
    G. Segmented animals have a fluid-filled coelum.
    H. Parts of some segments can become specialized to perform certain functions.
    J. Segments can evolve.
    K. Segments are separated by rings.

35. A group of worms other than the Annelida are called
    A. Lumbricus
    B. Nematodes
    C. Leeches
    D. Parapodia
    E. Metameres

36. Some annelid feet may be specialized in order to
    F. be used for locomotion.
    G. be segmented.
    H. be fluid-filled.
    J. evolve.
    K. grasp things.

37. A difference between the annelid coelum and the fluid-filled cavity of other worms is that
    A. the annelid coelum is involved in locomotion.
    B. the annelid coelum is formed later.
    C. the annelid coelum is formed during embryology.
    D. the annelid coelum is cylindrical in cross section.
    E. the annelid coelum separates the gut from the body wall.

38. An example of metameric specialization in the nervous system is
    F. segmental ganglia.
    G. the ventral nerve cord.
    H. respiratory organs.
    J. parpapodia
    K. cerebral ganglia

39. The main difference between the Annelida and all other animal phyla is that
    A. the Annelida are worms.
    B. the Annelida include the leeches.
    C. the Annelida are metameric.
    D. the Annelida are aquatic.
    E. the Annelida are specialized.

40. The purpose of the last paragraph in the passage is to
    F. give familiar examples of members of the annelid phylum.
    G. show that annelids may be parasites.
    H. tell the reader that annelids may be adapted to aquatic environments.
    J. show that there are many annelids in nature and that they are adapted to a wide variety of habitats.
    K. tell the reader that earthworms are annelids.

Science

Questions 1 and 2 are based upon the following figures and text:

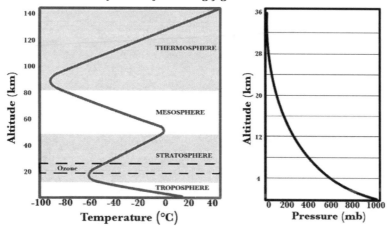

The Earth's atmosphere is comprised of multiple layers with very different temperature characteristics. Closest to the surface, the *troposphere* contains approximately 75 percent of the atmosphere's mass and 99 percent of its water vapor and aerosols. Temperature fluctuations cause constant mixing of air in the troposphere through convection, but it generally becomes cooler as altitude increases.

The *stratosphere* is heated by the absorption of ultraviolet radiation from the sun. Since its lower layers are composed of cooler, heavier air, there is no convective mixing in the stratosphere, and it is quite stable.

The *mesosphere* is the atmospheric layer directly above the stratosphere. Here, temperature decreases as altitude increases due to decreased solar heating and, to a degree, CO_2. In the lower atmosphere, CO_2 acts as a greenhouse gas by absorbing infrared radiation from the earth's surface. In the mesosphere, CO_2 cools the atmosphere by radiating heat into space.

Above this layer lies the *thermosphere*. At these altitudes, atmospheric gases form layers according to their molecular masses. Temperatures increase with altitude due to absorption of solar radiation by the small amount of residual oxygen. Temperatures are highly dependent on solar activity, and can rise to 1,500°C.

1. Commercial jetliners typically cruise at altitudes of 9-12 km, in the lower reaches of the stratosphere. Which of the following might be the reason for this choice of cruising altitude?
   A. Jet engines run more efficiently at colder temperatures.
   B. There is less air resistance than at lower altitudes.
   C. There is less turbulence than at lower altitudes.
   D. All of the above are possible reasons.

2. The lowest temperatures in the Earth's atmosphere are recorded within the:
   F. Troposphere
   G. Stratosphere
   H. Mesosphere
   J. Thermosphere

Questions 3 and 4 are based upon the following figure and text:

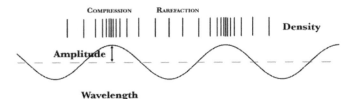

A vibrating source will produce sound by alternately forcing the air molecules in front of it closer together as it moves towards them, and then further apart as it draws away from them. In this way, alternating regions of high and low pressure, called compressions and refractions, are produced. The figure shows a typical sound wave. The volume of the sound corresponds to the magnitude of the compression, represented by the amplitude of the wave. The sound's pitch corresponds to the wave's frequency, the distance between successive compressions. Humans can hear sounds with frequencies between 20 and 20,000 Hertz. Sound waves propagate in all directions from their source. The speeds at which sound waves travel depend upon the medium they are traveling through. In dry air, sound travels at 330 m/sec at 0°C. It travels 4 times faster through water, and 15 times faster through a steel rod.

3. The sound produced by a drum is much louder and lower pitched than that produced by a bell. Which of the following statements is true about the sound wave produced by a drum compared to that produced by a bell?
   A. The amplitude is greater and the wavelength is shorter.
   B. The amplitude is greater and the wavelength is longer.
   C. The amplitude is smaller and the wavelength is longer.
   D. The amplitude is smaller and the wavelength is shorter.

4. Two sound waves of exactly the same frequency and amplitude are produced by sources that are in precisely the same position. If the sound waves are out of phase by one-half a wavelength, what will be heard by an observer standing a short distance away?
   F. A sound twice as loud as either individual signal
   G. A sound at twice the frequency of either individual signal
   H. A sound at twice the wavelength as either individual signal
   J. No sound at all

Questions 5 and 6 are based on the following figure and text:

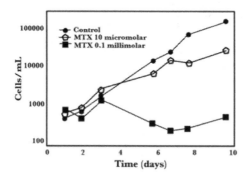

Cancer cells of the murine erythroleukemia (MEL) cell line were cultured in normal growth medium (control) and in two different concentrations of the anti-cancer drug methotrexate (MTX) for a period of ten days. Samples were removed periodically, and the number of cells per milliliter of culture was determined. Each point in the figure represents the mean of five determinations.

5. The growth of cells in the absence of drugs in this experiment can best be described as:
   A. Linear
   B. Exponential
   C. Derivative
   D. Inhibited

6. Which of the following statements is supported by the data?
   F. Methotrexate does not inhibit cell growth.
   G. 0.1 millimolar methotrexate inhibits the growth of bacteria.
   H. 10 micromolar methotrexate effectively suppresses cell growth.
   J. 100 micromolar methotrexate effectively suppresses cell growth.

7. The major advantage of sexual reproduction over asexual forms is that:
   A. It requires two individuals.
   B. It promotes diversity.
   C. It produces more offspring.
   D. It can be undertaken at any time of year.

Questions 8 and 9 are based on the following text:

<u>Isotopes</u>

The nucleus of an atom contains both protons and neutrons. Protons have a single positive electric charge, while neutrons have a charge of zero. The number of protons that a nucleus contains, called the atomic number and abbreviated as Z, determines the identity of an atom of matter. For example, hydrogen contains a single proton (Z =1), whereas helium contains two (Z = 2). Atoms of a single element may differ in terms of the number of neutrons in their atomic nuclei, however. The total number of protons and neutrons in an atom is referred to as the atomic mass, or M. Helium typically has an atomic mass equal to 4, but there is another helium isotope for which M = 3. This form of helium has the same number of protons, but only one neutron.

In an atomic fusion reaction, nuclei collide with one another with enough force to break them apart. The resulting nuclei may have a lower atomic mass than the reactants, with the difference being released as energy. Electric charge, however, is always conserved.

8. Two atoms of helium-3 (atomic mass = 3) collide in a fusion reaction to produce a single atom of helium-4 (atomic mass = 4). What might be another product of this reaction?
    F. A neutron
    G. A proton
    H. Two electrons
    J Two protons

9. Hydrogen atoms usually contain a single nucleon (nucleon refers to either a neutron or a proton). Deuterium and tritium are isotopes of hydrogen containing two and three nucleons, respectively. How many electrons orbit the tritium nucleus if the atom is electrically neutral?
    A. 0
    B. 1
    C. 2
    D. 3

Questions 10 and 11 are based on the following figure and text:

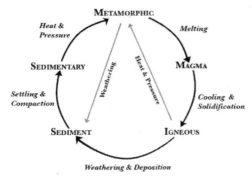

Rock Cycle
Rocks are created and destroyed in a recurrent process known as the rock cycle. Rocks are made from minerals, which are naturally occurring, crystalline solids of characteristic chemical composition. The actions of heat, pressure, and erosion can change the form of these minerals drastically. *Igneous* rocks form when molten magma is exuded from the Earth's molten core, and then cools and solidifies near the surface. *Sedimentary* rocks are made of fragments of other rocks worn by weathering or erosion. Sand particles form sediments as they settle to the bottom, and are eventually compacted into stone by the weight above them, a process called *lithification*. Heat and pressure can change the crystal structure of these minerals, altering them into denser *metamorphic* rocks, and as these sink deeper into the hot core, they melt again into magma.

10. A process that can lead to igneous rock formation is:
   F. Weathering
   G. Sedimentation
   H. Erosion
   J. Volcanic activity

11. Which of the following rock types is formed at the greatest distances below the Earth's surface?
   A. Igneous
   B. Metamorphic
   C. Sedimentary
   D. Slate

12. Which of the following animals displays the greatest fitness?
   F. A male wolf that dies young but has 4 cubs that are raised by an unrelated female
   G. A female wolf that has 3 cubs and lives to be quite old
   H. A male wolf that lives to old age and has 1 cub
   J. A female wolf that dies young after raising 3 cubs

Questions 13-18 are based upon the following figure, table, and text:

Protein Synthesis

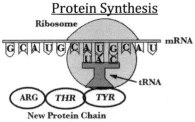

The Genetic Code

First	Codon	AA	Codon	AA	Codon	AA	Codon	AA
T	TTT	Phenylalanine	TCT	Serine	TAT	Tyrosine	TGT	Cysteine
	TTC	Phenylalanine	TCC	Serine	TAC	Tyrosine	TGC	Cysteine
	TTA	Leucine	TCA	Serine	TAA	STOP	TGA	STOP
	TTG	Leucine	TCG	Serine	TAG	STOP	TGG	Tryptophane
C	CTT	Leucine	CCT	Proline	CAT	Histidine	CGT	Arginine
	CTC	Leucine	CCC	Proline	CAC	Histidine	CGC	Arginine
	CTA	Leucine	CCA	Proline	CAA	Glycine	CGA	Arginine
	CTG	Leucine	CCG	Proline	CAG	Glycine	CGG	Arginine
A	ATT	Isoleucine	ACT	Threonine	AAT	Asparagine	AGT	Serine
	ATC	Isoleucine	ACC	Threonine	AAC	Asparagine	AGC	Serine
	ATA	Isoleucine	ACA	Threonine	AAA	Lysine	AGA	Arginine
	ATG	Methionine (START)	ACG	Threonine	AAG	Lysine	AGG	Arginine
G	GTT	Valine	GCT	Alanine	GAT	Aspartate	GGT	Glycine
	GTC	Valine	GCC	Alanine	GAC	Aspartate	GGC	Glycine
	GTA	Valine	GCA	Alanine	GAA	Glutamate	GGA	Glycine
	GTG	Valine	GCG	Alanine	GAG	Glutamate	GGG	Glycine

The genetic information for making different kinds of proteins is stored in segments of DNA molecules called genes. DNA is a chain of phosphoribose molecules containing the bases guanine (G), cytosine (C), alanine (A), and thymine (T). Each amino acid component of the protein chain is represented in the DNA by a trio of bases called a codon. This provides a code, which the cell can use to translate DNA into protein. The code, which is shown in the table, contains special codons for starting a protein chain (these chains always begin with the amino acid methionine), or for stopping it. To make a protein, an RNA intermediary called a messenger RNA (mRNA) is first made from the DNA by a protein called a polymerase. In the mRNA, the thymine bases are replaced by uracil (U). The mRNA then moves from the nucleus to the cytoplasm, where it locks onto a piece of protein-RNA machinery called a ribosome. The ribosome moves along the RNA molecule, reading the code. It interacts with molecules of transfer RNA, each of which is bound to a specific amino acid, and strings the amino acids together to form a protein.

13. Gene variants are called:
    A. Codons
    B. Alleles
    C. Methionine
    D. Amino acids

14. Which of the following protein sequences is encoded by the DNA base sequence GTTACAAAAAGA?
    F. Valine-threonine-lysine-arginine
    G. Valine-leucine-glycine-histidine
    H. Valine-aspartate-proline-serine
    J. Valine-serine-tyrosine-STOP

15. A polymerase begins reading the following DNA sequences with the first base shown. Which sequence specifies the end of a protein chain?
    A. GTACCCCTA
    B. GTACCCACA
    C. GTTAAAAGA
    D. GTTTAAGAC

16. The portion of a DNA molecule that encodes a single amino acid is a(n):
    F. Codon
    G. Allele
    H. Methionine
    J. Phosphoribose

17. Proteins are made by:
    A. Polymerases
    B. Transfer RNAs
    C. Ribosomes
    D. DNA molecules

18. Which of the following is NOT part of a gene?
    F. Guanine
    G. Codon
    H. Cytosine
    J. Ribosome

19. The pilot of an eastbound plane determines wind speed relative to his aircraft. He measures a wind velocity of 320 km/h, with the wind coming from the east. An observer on the ground sees the plane pass overhead, and measures its velocity as 290 km/h. What is the wind velocity relative to the observer?
    A. 30 km/h east-to-west
    B. 30 km/h west-to-east
    C. 320 km/h east-to-west
    D. 290 km/h east-to-west

Question 20 is based upon the following figure:

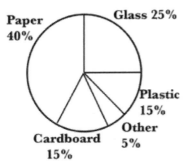

20. A recycling company collects sorted materials from its clients. The materials are weighed and then processed for re-use. The chart shows the weights of various classes of materials that were collected by the company during a representative month. Which of the following statements is NOT supported by the data in the chart?

F. Paper products, including cardboard, make up a majority of the collected materials.
G. One quarter of the materials collected are made of glass.
H. More plastic is collected than cardboard.
J. Plastic and cardboard together represent a larger portion of the collected materials than glass bottles.

21. During the process of oogenesis, primary oocytes produce:
A. Sperm
B. Eggs
C. Oogonia
E. None of the above

Questions 22-24 are based upon the following figure and text:
Electrochemical Battery

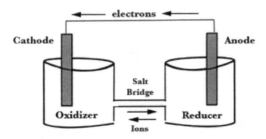

    An electrochemical battery is a device powered by oxidation and reduction reactions that are physically separated so that the electrons must travel through a wire from the reducing agent to the oxidizing agent. The reducing agent loses electrons, and is oxidized in a reaction that takes place at an electrode called the anode. The electrons flow through a wire to the other electrode, the cathode, where an oxidizing agent gains electrons and is thus reduced. To maintain a net zero charge in each compartment, there is a limited flow of ions through a salt bridge. In a car battery, for example, the reducing agent is oxidized by the following reaction, which involves a lead (Pb) anode and sulfuric acid (H_2SO_4). Lead sulfate ($PbSO_4$), protons (H^+), and electrons (e^-) are produced:

$$Pb + H_2SO_4 \Rightarrow PbSO_4 + 2\ H^+ + 2\ e^-$$

- 114 -

At the cathode, which is made of lead oxide (PbO_2), the following reaction occurs. During this reaction, the electrons produced at the anode are used:

$$PbO_2 + H_2SO_4 + 2\ e^- + 2\ H^+ \Rightarrow PbSO_4 + 2\ H_2O$$

22. Electrons are produced by a chemical reaction that takes place at the:
    F. Anode
    G. Cathode
    H. Lead oxide electrode
    J. Oxidizer

23. In an oxidation reaction:
    A. An oxidizing agent gains electrons.
    B. An oxidizing agent loses electrons.
    C. A reducing agent gains electrons.
    D. A reducing agent loses electrons.

24. In a car battery, a product of the oxidation reaction that occurs at the cathode is:
    F. Lead oxide
    G. Lead
    H. Electrons
    J. Water

Questions 25-26 are based upon the following figure:

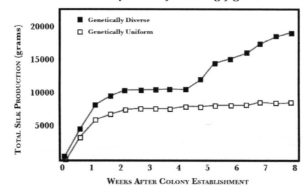

25. Colonies of silkworms containing the same number of genetically identical or genetically varying animals were established. For several weeks after the colonies were created, silk production was estimated by removing small samples of silk from the colonies and weighing them. The results are shown in the graph. The open symbols refer to the production of silk by genetically uniform worms, while the closed symbols refer to production of silk by genetically diverse worms. Which of the following conclusions can be drawn from the data?
    A. Genetically diverse worms produce more silk than genetically uniform worms.
    B. Genetically uniform worms produce more silk than genetically diverse worms.
    C. Genetically diverse silkworm colonies produce more silk than genetically uniform colonies.
    D. Genetically uniform silkworm colonies produce more silk than genetically diverse colonies.

26. If the generation time of a silkworm is about four weeks, which of the following hypotheses offers the best explanation for the difference in silk productivity between the two colonies?

F. Genetically diverse silkworms produce silk longer than genetically uniform worms.
G. Genetically diverse silkworms reproduce more than genetically uniform worms.
H. Genetically diverse silkworms produce heavier silk than genetically uniform worms.
J. Genetically uniform silkworms stop producing silk when they reproduce.

27. The digestion of starch begins:

A. In the mouth
B. In the stomach
C. In the pylorus
D. In the duodenum

Questions 28-31 are based upon the following figure and text:

THE WATER CYCLE

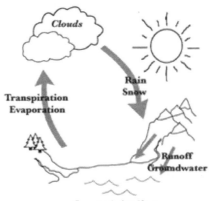

Energy from the sun heats the water in the oceans and causes it to evaporate, forming water vapor that rises through the atmosphere. Cooler temperatures at high altitudes cause this vapor to condense and form clouds. Water droplets in the clouds condense and grow, eventually falling to the ground as precipitation. This continuous movement of water above and below ground is called the hydrologic cycle, or water cycle, and it is essential for life on our planet. All the Earth's stores of water, including that found in clouds, oceans, underground, etc., are known as the *hydrosphere*.

Water can be stored in several locations as part of the water cycle. The largest reservoirs are the oceans, which hold about 95% of the world's water, more than 300,000,000 cubic miles. Water is also stored in polar ice caps, mountain snowcaps, lakes and streams, plants, and below ground in aquifers. Each of these reservoirs has a characteristic *residence time*, which is the average amount of time a water molecule will spend there before moving on. Some typical residence times are shown in the table.

Average reservoir residence times of water.

Reservoir	Residence Time
Atmosphere	days 9
Oceans	3000 years
Glaciers and ice caps	years 100
Soil moisture	months 2
Underground aquifers	10,000 years

The water cycle can change over time. During cold climatic periods, more water is stored as ice and snow, and the rate of evaporation is lower. This affects the level of the Earth's oceans. During the last ice age, for instance, oceans were 400 feet lower than today. Human activities that affect the water cycle include agriculture, dam construction, deforestation, and industrial activities.

28. Another name for the water cycle is:
    F. The hydrosphere
    G. The atmosphere
    H. The reservoir
    J. The hydrologic cycle

29. Water is stored underground, as well as in oceans and ice caps. Such underground storage reservoirs are called:
    A. Storage tanks
    B. Aquifers
    C. Evaporators
    D. Runoff

30. Other than atmospheric water, water molecules spend the least time in:
    F. Aquifers
    G. Oceans
    H. Glaciers
    J. Soil

31. Which of the following statements is NOT true?
    A. Cutting down trees affects the water cycle.
    B. Ocean levels rise during an ice age.
    C. Oceans hold most of the world's water.
    D. Clouds are formed because of cold temperatures.

Questions 32-36 are based upon the following figure and text:
<u>Heat and the States of Matter</u>

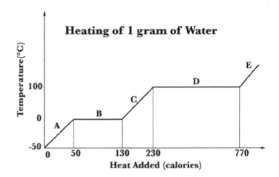

When the molecules of a substance absorb energy in the form of heat, they begin to move more rapidly. This increase in kinetic energy may be a more rapid vibration of molecules held in place in a solid, or it may be motion through molecular space in a liquid or a gas. Either way, it will be observed as either a change in temperature or a change in state. Heat has traditionally been measured in terms of calories. One calorie is equal to 4.186 Joules.

The specific heat capacity of a substance is the energy required to raise the temperature of 1 kg of the substance by 1°C. For water, this is 1000 calories. If heat continues to be applied to ice that is already at its melting point of 0°C, it remains at that temperature and melts into liquid water. The amount of energy required to produce this change in state is called the heat of fusion, and for water it is equal to 80 calories per gram. Similarly, the amount of energy required to change a gram of liquid water at 100°C into steam is called the heat of vaporization, and equals 540 calories.

The graph shows an experiment in calorimetry: 1 gram of water at -50°C is heated slowly from a solid state until it has all turned to gas. The temperature is monitored and reported as a function of the heat added to the system.

32. Heat is a form of:
    F. Potential energy
    G. Chemical energy
    H. Kinetic energy
    J. Temperature

33. Which of the following statements is true?
    A. Adding heat to a system always increases its temperature.
    B. The average speed of a gas molecule is slower than the average speed of a liquid molecule of the same substance.
    C. Adding heat to a system always increases the average speed of the molecules of which it is comprised.
    D. Heat must be added to liquid water to make ice.

34. In the diagram, in which region(s) of the diagram is liquid water present?
   F. B only
   G. B and C
   H. C only
   J. B, C, and D

35. How much heat must be added to 1 gram of water at 1°C to raise its temperature to 101°C?
   A. 100 calories
   B. 540 calories
   C. 770 calories
   D. 640 calories

36. In the diagram, as heat is added to the system, the water in region B can be said to be:
   F. Condensing
   G. Melting
   H. Freezing
   J. Evaporating

Question 37 is based upon the following figure:

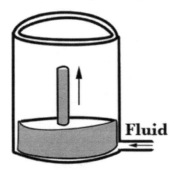

37. The figure shows an airtight cylinder into which fluid may be injected from the bottom. The cylinder contains a heavy piston which is raised by the injected fluid until the rod on top of the piston touches the top of the cylinder container. Fluids of different densities are injected, and an observer records the volume required to make the rod reach the top. Which of the following fluids will require the least injected volume?
   A. Water
   B. Oil
   C. Alcohol
   D. The same volume will be required for all fluids.

38. Mark and Nancy both measure the length of a pencil that is 15.1 cm. They use a ruler that has divisions for every mm along its length. Mark reports the length of the pencil as 15 cm. Nancy reports it as 15.0 cm. Which of the following statements is true?
   F. Mark's measurement is more precise.
   G. Nancy's measurement is more accurate.
   H. Mark's measurement is more accurate.
   J. Nancy's measurement is more precise.

Questions 39-40 are based upon the following figure:

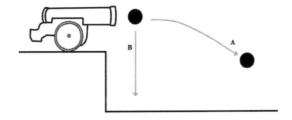

39. A cannon sits on top of a cliff 20 meters above an expanse of level ground. It fires a 5 kg cannonball horizontally (cannonball A) at 5 meters/second. At the same time, a second cannonball (cannonball B) is dropped from the same height. If air resistance is negligible, which cannonball will hit the ground first?
Note: The gravitational acceleration due to the Earth is 9.8 m/sec².
    A. Cannonball A
    B. Cannonball B
    C. Both will hit the ground at the same time.
    D. It will depend upon the temperature.

40. The cannon weighs 500 kg and is on wheels. It will recoil as a result of firing cannonball A. If friction is negligible, what will be the recoil speed of the cannon? Note: Momentum is the product of mass and velocity.
    F. 5 meters/second
    G. 5000 cm/second
    H. 50 cm/second
    J. 5 cm/second

Writing

The city council has raised the issue of setting a curfew for children under the age of 17 to keep young drivers off the road after a certain time at night. They know it is legal, but still plan to discuss it at the next meeting, including whether the idea is worthwhile, whether the curfew would be all the time or only on school nights, and whether or not the age of 17 is too high. The subject will be open for ideas.

Write an essay. Discuss your position on the curfew issue. In your essay, select either of these points of view, or suggest an alternative approach, and make a case for it. Use specific reasons and appropriate examples to support your position and to show how it is superior to the others.

Answer Key and Explanations

English

Number	Answer	Number	Answer	Number	Answer
1	D	26	G	51	D
2	H	27	C	52	G
3	A	28	H	53	C
4	G	29	B	54	G
5	B	30	J	55	D
6	H	31	C	56	G
7	A	32	G	57	C
8	H	33	D	58	F
9	D	34	H	59	C
10	F	35	B	60	G
11	D	36	J	61	C
12	G	37	C	62	J
13	B	38	H	63	B
14	H	39	C	64	J
15	D	40	F	65	D
16	H	41	B	66	F
17	D	42	H	67	B
18	G	43	A	68	F
19	B	44	H	69	D
20	G	45	C	70	G
21	C	46	J	71	B
22	G	47	B	72	G
23	D	48	H	73	C
24	H	49	B	74	J
25	B	50	H	75	C

1. D: The correct verb tense in this sentence is the past perfect tense with "gone" rather than "went."

2. H: "Their" is the correct word when indicating a possessive form of they.

3. A: This sentence correctly uses the possessive case.

4. G: As a car is something people enter rather than sit on top of, the correct answer is the one that indicates that the family, in the past, got into the car.

5. B: Equipment should be singular.

6. H: The option is the correct form of the possessive case for a singular noun (Lucy).

7. A: This sentence as written correctly uses the possessive form of they.

8. H: "Too" is the correct spelling of the word meaning also.

9. D: "Next to Ella" is the grammatically correct way to indicate this physical proximity.

10. F: The sentence is correct as written.

11. D: The tense needed here is past perfect progressive (indicating ongoing action completed at a definite time). Answer D is the only option with the correct tense.

12. G: The action happened in the past so the correct verb tense is "pulled." One gets off a highway rather than of a highway.

13. B: Need the indication of past tense that the "were" provides.

14. H: One fills in a crossword puzzle, rather than files in a crossword puzzle.

15. D: The action happened in the past, so the past tense version of the verb is correct.

16. H: One eats their food rather than drinks it.

17. D: The action happened in the past, so the past tense version of the verb is correct.

18. G: The verb forms should be parallel.

19. B: The phrase occurred in the past so "fell" is the correct verb tense. Quick needs to be in the form of an adverb to modify the verb fell, so "quickly" is correct.

20. G: The sentence is awkward and doesn't make sense as written. It makes sense if the sentence is written so that the two actions happen simultaneously.

21. C: The action happened in the past, so the past tense version of the verb is correct.

22. G: The only correct verb form of the options given is woke up.

23. D: The correct expression is "out of" when one is removing something from a container.

24. H: The action happened in the past, so the past tense version of the verb is correct.

25. B: The possessive form of it is its.

26. G: The correct expression is wide awake.

27. C: The word sought must be a noun and surprise fits the context better than stupor.

28. H: The verb tense needed is past perfect, indicating a completed action.

29. B: The correct spelling of the fruit is "plum."

30. J: The sentence requires a noun that one experiences when feeling resigned. The correct word is resignation.

31. C: The correct verb tense in this sentence is the present perfect because it refers to a state of being that began in the past (they got married) but is not yet finished (they are still married).

32. G: The correct word is "their." This word is a plural possessive form of "they," whereas the word "there" refers to a place.

33. D: The verb "to go" is irregular. The correct tense here is the past simple, "went," instead of the past perfect, "had gone," because the sentence refers to only one finished past action.

34. H: The correct verb tense is the past simple "they arrived" instead of the past continuous "they were arriving."

35. B: The correct form should be the infinitive plus an -ing verb. The main verb in the sentence, swerved, tells us the action happened in the past.

36. J: Carla is a noun that does not end in "s," so the possessive is formed by adding an apostrophe and s, as in "Carla's."

37. C: The verb to fly is an irregular verb; the correct form of the past tense is "flew."

38. H: This word needs to be in the form of an adverb; the correct spelling is "angrily."

39. C: The past tense of the word "can" is "could," so the correct answer is "could find."

40. F: This sentence uses the correct verb tense. The past perfect is used because it refers to a past action that happened before another past action.

41. B: The correct spelling of the word is "apologetically."

42. H: This sentence should use the contraction "it's," meaning "it is." The word "its" refers to the singular possessive.

43. A: This sentence correctly uses the word "there."

44. H: The correct relative pronoun to use in this relative clause is "who," because the pronoun is referring to a person and is not possessive.

45. C: The correct word to use in this sentence is "too," which means "also."

46. J: The verb "to wake" is irregular and the past tense is "woke."

47. B: The correct prepositional phrase to use here is "to the beach."

48. H: The verb "to catch" is irregular and the past tense is "caught." "Fish" is an uncountable noun and the plural form is the same as the singular form, so no "s" is added to make it plural.

49. B: The present form of the verb is used here, because the main verb in this phrase is in the past simple, so the second verb should use the infinitive.

50. H: The verb should be in the past simple form and not the past perfect, since this action (got stung) happened after the first action in the sentence (had stepped).

51. D: The verb tense should be past simple. Past perfect is not needed here because the actions mentioned in the sentence happened one after another in sequence.

52. G: The correct prepositional phrase is "in the room."

53. C: The correct tense should be past simple (realized) followed by past perfect (had left), because there are two actions and the second action happened before the first action.

54. G: This is the wrong word. The correct verb is "pour" which means to rain hard.

55. D: The correct verb tense should be past perfect because the action happened before this other action in the past.

56. G: The correct verb should be singular, "was soaked," because "everything" is a collective singular noun.

57. C: The correct verb is "were," because it refers to three items, not just one. The correct spelling of the verb "ruin" in the past tense is "ruined."

58. F: This sentence correctly uses the verb and preposition.

59. C: The verb in this sentence, "to go," should use the past simple form, "went." "Gone" is the past participle of "to go."

60. G: The correct spelling of the word is "unsuccessful."

61. C: This employs the past participle "have colored".

62. J: Using the past tense of "to use".

63. B: The end of the sentence is not a separate clause and should not be separated by a comma.

64. J: "Dying" means to end life, while "dyeing" means to color a fabric. "Variously" is an adverb that should modify a verb, not the noun "techniques".

65. D: The subject is singular and the context calls for a verb in the past tense.

66. F

67. B: Which uses a comma to set off a subordinate clause.

68. F

69. D: Choice A is slang.

70. G: "To comprise" means "to be composed of".

71. B: Choice A is slang.

72. G: Choices J and K have inappropriate commas.

73. C: Which exhibits the standard word order of subject – verb – indirect object.

74. J: Which reads most smoothly using the prepositional phrase "long before".

75. C: Choices A and B are awkwardly phrased.

Mathematics

Number	Answer	Number	Answer	Number	Answer
1	D	21	D	41	E
2	J	22	G	42	G
3	D	23	C	43	E
4	F	24	G	44	F
5	D	25	D	45	D
6	G	26	K	46	K
7	A	27	D	47	B
8	G	28	G	48	F
9	D	29	A	49	A
10	J	30	H	50	G
11	B	31	A	51	A
12	F	32	F	52	J
13	E	33	D	53	C
14	H	34	H	54	H
15	D	35	C	55	B
16	H	36	G	56	K
17	A	37	C	57	C
18	F	38	H	58	J
19	D	39	D	59	B
20	K	40	J	60	J

1. D: Jamie had $2.75 after all of the transactions described. To solve this problem, first subtract $4.25 and $2.00 from the initial sum of $6.50, leaving $0.25. Then, add $2.50, arriving at the final answer of $2.75.

2. J: There are two ways to solve this problem: either convert meters to centimeters and then use the conversion factor in the table to convert centimeters to inches, or use the table to convert meters to yards, and then convert to inches.

In the first instance, recall that there are 100 centimeters in a meter (*centi* means "hundredth"). Therefore, 19 m = 1900 cm = $(\frac{1900}{2.54})$ = 748 inches.

In the second instance, recall that there are 36 inches in a yard, therefore 19 m = 19 x 1.094 = 20.786 yd = 20.786 x 36 = 748 inches.

Proportions are commonly used for conversions. After converting meters to centimeters, set up proportions to solve for an unknown variable, *x*.

$(\frac{1900}{x})cm/in = 2.54cm/in$ Cross multiply.

2.54*x* = 1900   Divide each side by 2.54 to solve for *x*.
x = 748 inches

3. D: Since 16 chairs are empty, and this represents 2/5 of the total enrollment, then the full class must consist of

Class = $\frac{5}{2} \times 16 = 40$ students.

Use proportions:

$\frac{2}{5} = \frac{16}{x}$ Cross multiply.

$2x = 80$ Divide each side by 2 to solve for x.

$x = 40$ students.

4. F: Begin by determining the total cost of the onions and carrots, since these prices are given. This will equal (2 x $3.69) + (3 x $4.29) = $20.25. Next, this sum is subtracted from the total cost of the vegetables to determine the cost of the mushrooms: $24.15 - $20.25 = $3.90. Finally, the cost of the mushrooms is divided by the quantity (lbs) to determine the cost per pound:

Cost per lb = $\frac{\$3.90}{1.5} = \$2.60$.

5. D: Since the figure represents the number line, the distance from point A to point B will be the difference, B-A, which is 5 – (-6) = 11. The distance from point B to point C will be the difference, C-B, which is 8 – 5 = 3. So, the ratio BC:AB will be 3:11.

6. G: If the first lap takes 50 seconds, the second one takes 20% more, or $T_2 = 1.2 \times T_1 = 1.2 \times 50 = 60$ seconds, where T_1 and T_2 are the times required for the first and second laps, respectively. Similarly, $T_3 = 1.2 \times T_2 = 1.2 \times 60 = 72$ seconds, the time required for the third lap. To find the total time, add the times for the three laps together: 50 + 60 + 72 = 182 seconds.

7. A: Candidate A's vote percentage is determined by the number of votes that he obtained, divided by the total number of votes cast, and then multiplied by 100 to convert the decimal into a percentage. Therefore,

Candidate A's vote percentage $= \frac{36800}{36800+32100+2100} \times 100 = 51.8\%$.

8. G: The easiest pair to test is the third: $y = 4$ and $x = 0$. Substitute these values into each of the given equations and evaluate. Choice G gives 4 = 0 + 4, which is a true statement. None of the other answer choices are correct using this number set.

9. D: At the point of intersection, the y-coordinates are equal on both lines so that $2x+3 = x-5$. Solving for x, we have $x = -8$. Then, evaluating y with either equation yields $y = 2(-8)+3 = -16+3 = -13$, or $y = -8-5 = -13$.

10. J: The perimeter (P) of the quadrilateral is simply the sum of its sides, or $P = m+(m+2)+(m+3)+2m$.
Combine like terms by adding the variables (m terms) together, and then adding the constants, resulting in $P = 5m+5$.

Note: In this application, it appears that some of the variables do not have a number in front of them. However, the absence of a coefficient indicates that they are multiplied by 1, such as $m = 1m$, $x = 1x$, and so on.

11. B: Divide David's total profit of $22.00 by the number of shares he purchased, 200, to determine David's profit per share:
$P = \$22.00 \div 200 = \$0.11$, or 11¢ per share.
So, the price he paid was 11¢ lower than the closing price shown in the table. Since the table shows that Oracle closed at $19.11 per share today, the price David paid was $19.11 - $0.11 = $19.00 per share.

12. F: Evaluate as follows: $2f(x) - 3 = 2(2x^2 + 7) - 3 = 4x^2 + 14 - 3 = 4x^2 + 11$.

13. E: The stock first increased by 10%, or $10 (10% of $100), to $110 per share. Then, the price decreased by $11 (10% of $110), so that the sell price was $110 – $11 = $99 per share, and the sell price for 50 shares was 99 x $50 = $4950.

14. H: The longest side of a right triangle, called the hypotenuse, H, can be calculated using the Pythagorean Theorem, together with the lengths of the other two sides, which are given as 6 and 8 units: $H^2 = S_1^2 + S_2^2 = 6^2 + 8^2 = 36 + 64 = 100$, $\sqrt{H^2} = \sqrt{100}$, $H = 10$. Therefore, using $H = 10$, the perimeter, P, can be calculated as follows: $P = 10 + 6 + 8 = 24$.

15. D: First, add the two straight, 150-yard portions. Also, note that the distance around the two semi-circular turns combine to form the circumference of a circle. The radius, r, of that circle is ½ of the dimension that is shown as the width of the track, or 15 yards. Now, taking the formula for the circumference of a circle, $2\pi r$, and adding it to the length of the two straight portions of the track, we have
$Length = (2\pi \times 15) + (2 \times 150) = 394.25$.
Answer D is the closest approximation to this calculated answer.

16. H: First, determine the total distance of the round trip. This is twice the 45 miles of the one-way trip to work in the morning, which equals 90 miles. Then, determine the total amount of time that Elijah spent on his round trip by converting his travel times into minutes. 1-hour-and-10-minutes is equivalent to 70 minutes, and 1-hour-and-30-minutes is equivalent to 90 minutes. Thus, Elijah's total travel time was 70 + 90 = 160 minutes. Elijah's average speed can now be determined in miles per minute:
$Speed = \dfrac{90\,miles}{160\,min} = 0.5625\,miles$ per minute.
Finally, to convert this average speed into miles per hour, multiply by 60, since there are 60 minutes in an hour:
Average speed (mph) = 60 x 0.5625 = 33.75 miles per hour.

17. A: The area of a triangle equals half of the product of the base x height. Since the base passes through the center, we have base = $2r$ and height = r, so that the area A is
$A = \dfrac{r \times 2r}{2} = r^2$

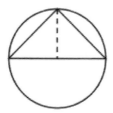

18. F: The rate of increase equals the change in the account balance divided by the original amount, $80. Multiply that decimal by 100 to yield the percentage of increase. To determine the change in the balance, subtract the original amount from the new balance:
$Change = \$120 - \$80 = \$40.$
Now, determine the percentage of increase as described above:
$Percent = \dfrac{\$40}{\$80} \times 100 = 50\%.$

19. D: The probability of getting three aces in a row is the product of the probabilities for each draw. For the first ace, that is 4 in 52, since there are 4 aces in a deck of 52 cards. For the second, it is 3 in 51, since 3 aces and 51 cards remain; and for the third, it is 2 in 50. So, the overall probability, P, is $P = \frac{4}{52} \times \frac{3}{51} \times \frac{2}{50} = \frac{24}{132600} = \frac{1}{5525}$.

20. K: Begin as you would a regular equation:

$4x - 12 < 4$ Add 12 to each side.
$4x < 16$ Divide by 4.
$x < 4$

     Note: The inequality does not change because the division was by *positive* 4.
     Since x must be less than 4, and not equal to it ($<$ not $\leq$), the answer J is incorrect: the
     solution does not include 4. Only answer K satisfies the condition that it must be < 4.

21. D: First, compute the value enclosed by the parentheses, $3b + 5 = 3 \times 7 + 5 = 26$. Next, compute $4a = -24$. Note that a is negative, so this product is also negative. The product, $4a(3b + 5)$, will therefore be negative, as well, and equals -624. Finally, add the value of $2b$, or 2 x 7 = 14, to -624, to get the final answer: $624 + 14 = -610$.
Substitute the given values for the variables into the expression:
$4 \times -6(3 \times 7 + 5) + 2 \times 7$
Using the order of operations, compute the expression in the parentheses first. Remember that you must first multiply 3 by 7, and then add 5, in order to follow order of operations.
= $4 \times -6(21 + 5) + 2 \times 7$ Next add the values in the parentheses.
= $4 \times -6(26) + 2 \times 7$ Simplify by multiplying the numbers outside of the parentheses.
= $-24(26) + 14$ Multiply -24 by 26.
= $-624 + 14$ Add.
= -610

22. G: Since the rate, in miles per minute, is constant, this can be solved by setting up a proportion: $\dfrac{miles}{min} = \dfrac{10}{12} = \dfrac{210}{t}$. Now, solve for time: $t = \dfrac{210 \times 12}{10} = 252$ minutes. Finally,

convert to hours by dividing this total by 60, since there are 60 minutes in an hour:

$t = \dfrac{252}{60} = 4$ hours and 12 minutes.

Note: When dividing 252 by 60, you get a decimal answer: 4.2 hours. However, the answers are represented in a different unit of measurement: 4.2 hours is neither 4 hours and 2 minutes, nor is it 4 hours and 20 minutes. In order to find the number of minutes, the decimal (0.2) has to be converted into minutes. To convert to minutes, multiply 0.2 by 60, which yields 12 minutes.

23. C: Define the variable t as the elapsed time (in hours) from the time the first airplane takes off. Then, at any time, the distance traveled by the first plane is $d_1 = 250t$. The second plane takes off 30 minutes later, so that, at any time, the distance that it has traveled is $d_2 = 280(t - 30)$. This plane will overtake the first when the two distances are equal, which is when $d_1 = d_2$, or when $250t = 280(t - 30)$. First, use the distributive property to solve for t: $250t = 280t - 8400$.
Next, add 8400 to each side of the equation: $250t + 8400 = 280t$.
Next, subtract $250t$ from each side of the equation: $8400 = 30t$.
Next, divide both sides by 30: $t = 280$.

This gives the value of t in minutes. Convert to hours by dividing 280 by 60 minutes per hour, which yields an elapsed time of 4 hours and 40 minutes (remember to multiply the decimal (0.66) by 60 in order to convert the decimal into minutes (40 min)). Since the first plane left at 2 PM, 4 hours and 40 minutes later is 6:40 PM.

24. G: Since the figure is a right triangle, the Pythagorean Theorem may be applied. The side that is 25 units long is the hypotenuse, and its square will equal the sum of the squares of the other two sides. That is, $25^2 = 15^2 + x^2$. Solve for x^2 by subtracting 15^2 from each side of this equation, and then take the square root to determine x:

$$x = \sqrt{25^2 - 15^2} = \sqrt{625 - 225} = \sqrt{400} = 20.$$

25. D: Since each of the 3 models is available in each of the 6 different colors, there are 6 x 3 = 18 different combinations available. If we label the models as A, B, and C, and the colors as 1 through 6, then the combinations can be broken down as follows:

Models	Colors	
Model A	A1 A2 A3 A4 A5 A6	
Model B	B1 B2 B3 B4 B5 B6	
Model C	C1 C2 C3 C4 C5 C6	=18 Total Combinations

This method is more time consuming. However, it provides a visual representation as to why the total number of combinations is based on the product.

26. K: First, test each expression to see which satisfies the condition $x > y$. This condition is met for all the answer choices except H and J, so these need not be considered further. Next, test the remaining choices to see which satisfy the inequality $x + y > 0$. It can be seen that this inequality holds for choices F and G, but not for choice K, since $x + y = 3 + (-3) = 3 - 3 = 0$. In this case the sum $x + y$ is not greater than 0.

27. D: In order to multiply two powers that have the same base, add their exponents. Therefore, $x^3 x^5 = x^{3+5} = x^8$.

Also note that $x^3 = x \cdot x \cdot x$. Therefore, the expression equals $x \cdot x \cdot x \cdot x \cdot x \cdot x \cdot x \cdot x$.

28. G: A proportion such as this can be solved by taking the cross product of the numerators and denominators from either side.

$$\frac{12}{x} = \frac{30}{6}$$ Take the cross product by cross multiplication.

$30x = 6 \times 12$ Multiply 6 by 12.

$30x = 72$ Divide each side by 30.

$x = 2.4$

29. A: This is a typical plot of an inverse variation, in which the product of the dependent and independent variables, x and y, is always equal to the same value. In this case, the product is always equal to 1, so the plot occupies the first and third quadrants of the coordinate plane. As x increases and approaches infinity, y decreases and approaches zero, maintaining the constant product. In contrast, answer B is a linear plot, corresponding to an equation of the form $y = x$. C is a quadratic plot corresponding to $y = x^2$. D is an exponential plot corresponding to $y = 2^x$. And, E is another linear plot corresponding to

$$y = \frac{x}{4} + 1.$$

30. H: The internal angles of a triangle always add up to 180°. Since $\triangle ABC$ is a right triangle, then $\angle ABC = 90°$, and $\angle ACB$ is given as 30°. The middle letter represents the vertex. By using the triangle addition theorem, the answer must be: $\angle BAC = 180 - (90+30)$, which equals 60°.

31. A: This equation represents a linear relationship that has a slope of 3.60, and passes through the origin. The table indicates that for each hour of rental, the cost increases by $3.60. This corresponds to the slope of the equation. Of course, if the bicycle is not rented at all (0 hours), there will be no charge ($0). If plotted on the Cartesian plane, the line would have a y intercept of 0. Therefore, relationship A is the only one that satisfies these criteria.

32. F: Complementary angles are two angles that equal 90° when added together.

33. D: The slopes of perpendicular lines are reciprocals of opposite signs. For example, in the figure below, line A has a slope of -1/2, while line B has a slope of 2.

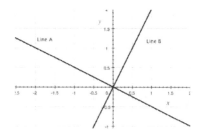

34. H: To see this, consider the following table, which shows the numbers of coins added to the first few squares, and the equivalent powers of 2:

Square	1	2	3	4
Coins	1	2	4	8
Power of 2	2^0	2^1	2^2	2^3

The table shows that, in this series, the number of coins on each square represents consecutive powers of 2, since the number doubles with each consecutive square. However, the series of powers begins with 0 for the first square, so that, for the 64th square, the number of coins will be 2^{63}.

35. C: Since there are four different colors, one color must be excluded from each balloon bundle. Therefore, there is one color set for each excluded color, or four in all. This problem can also be solved mathematically, as follows. An arrangement such as this, in which the order of the individual components is not important, is called a combination. The number of combinations of n objects taken k at a time is given by $C = \dfrac{n!}{(n-k)!k!}$. The ! notation indicates a *factorial* product, where $n! = 1 \times 2 \times 3 \times \ldots \times (n-1) \times n$. In this case, n = 4 colors, and k = 3 balloons per bundle. Substituting into the equation above, and simplifying, yields:
$$C = \frac{4!}{(4-3)!3!} = \frac{1 \times 2 \times 3 \times 4}{(1)(1 \times 2 \times 3)} = 4$$

36. G: The two right triangles are similar because they share a pair of vertical angles. Vertical angles are always congruent ($\angle ACB$ and $\angle DCE$). Obviously, both right angles ($\angle ABC$ and $\angle CDE$) are congruent. Thus, $\angle BAC$ and $\angle DEC$ are congruent because of the triangular sum theorem.
With similar triangles, corresponding sides will be proportional. Segment BC is ½ the length of segment CD, and therefore AC will be ½ the length of CE. The length of CE can be computed from the Pythagorean Theorem, since it is the hypotenuse of a right triangle in which the lengths of the other two sides are known: $CE = \sqrt{6^2 + 8^2} = \sqrt{100} = 10$.
The length of segment AC will be ½ of this value, or 5 units.

37. C: This can be solved as two equations with two unknowns. Since the integers are consecutive, with $p > n$, we have $p - n = 1$, so that $p = 1 + n$. Substituting this value into $p + n = 15$ gives $1 + 2n = 15$, or $n = \dfrac{14}{2} = 7$.

38. H: For each die, there is 1 chance in 6 that a 6 will emerge on top, since the die has 6 sides. The probability that a 6 will show for each die is not affected by the results obtained for any other. Since these probabilities are independent, the overall probability of throwing 3 sixes is the product of the individual probabilities, or
$$P = \frac{1}{6} \times \frac{1}{6} \times \frac{1}{6}$$
$$= \frac{1}{6^3}$$
$$= \frac{1}{216}$$

39. D: Rafael's profit on each computer is given by the difference between the price he pays and the price he charges his customer, or $800-$450. If he sells n computers in a month, his total profit will be n times this difference, or $n(800-450)$. However, it is necessary to subtract his fixed costs of $3000 from this to compute his final profit per month.

40. J: When a number is raised to a power, it is multiplied by itself as many times as the power indicates. For example, $2^3 = 2 \times 2 \times 2 = 8$. A number raised to the power of 0 is always equal to 1, so 6^0 is the smallest number shown. Similarly, the other numbers can be transformed as follows: $9 = 9^1 = 9$; $10^1 = 10$; $4^2 = 4 \times 4 = 16$.

41. E: The area of the circle is πr^2, while the circumference is $2\pi r$. Taking the ratio of these two expressions and reducing gives $Ratio = \dfrac{\pi r^2}{2\pi r} = \dfrac{r}{2}$.

42. G: The figure is a pie chart, a circular diagram that shows the relative amounts of each variable as a slice of the whole circle. The larger the variable: the larger the slice. In addition, the percentage of each variable, or recycled material, is shown next to each slice. In this chart, paper is the most common recycled material, or the largest variable, representing 40% of the total. The next largest is glass, at 25% of the total. All of the other materials represent smaller portions of the total.

43. E: The chart indicates that 40% of the total recycled material is paper. Since 50,000 tons of materials are recycled every month, the total amount of paper will be 40% of 50,000 tons, or $\dfrac{40}{100} \times 50,000 = 20,000$ tons.

44. F: Let D represent Dorothy's age, and S her sister's age. Since she is half of her sister's age today, we have $D = \dfrac{S}{2}$, or $S = 2D$. In twenty years, her age will be $D + 20$ years, and her sister's age will be $S + 20$ years. At that time, Dorothy will be ¾ of her sister's age. Therefore, $D + 20 = \dfrac{3 \times (S + 20)}{4}$. Substituting $2D$ for S in this equation gives

$$D + 20 = \frac{3(2D + 20)}{4}$$

$$D + 20 = \frac{6D + 60}{4}$$

Use the Distributive property and reduce.

$$D + 20 = \frac{3}{2}D + 15$$

$$D + 20 = \frac{3D}{2} + 15$$

Gathering like terms:

$$20 - 15 = \frac{3D}{2} - D,\text{ which is equivalent to } 5 = \frac{D}{2}.$$

Therefore, $D = 10$ years old. Dorothy is ten years old today, and her sister is twenty years old. In twenty years, Dorothy will be 30 years old, and her sister will be 40 years old.

45. D: Remember that, when you multiply like bases, you add the exponents; and, when you divide like bases, you subtract the exponents. Thus,
$(xy)^{7y} - (xy)^y = (xy)^y[(xy)^{6y} - 1]$.

46. K: It is not necessary to use the circle formula to solve the problem. Rather, note that 50 km/hr corresponds to 50,000 meters per hour. We are given the tire's revolutions per minute, and the answer must be represented as meters. Therefore, the speed must be converted to meters per minute. This corresponds to a speed of $\dfrac{50{,}000}{60}$ meters per minute, as there are 60 minutes in an hour. In addition, in any given minute, the tires rotate 500 times around, and hence 500 times its circumference. This corresponds to $\dfrac{50{,}000}{60 \times 500} = \dfrac{10}{6}$ meters per revolution, which is the circumference of the tire.

47. B: In this probability problem, there are three independent events (the codes for each digit), each with ten possible outcomes (the numerals 0-9). Since the events are independent, the total possible outcomes is equal to the product of the possible outcomes for each of the three events, that is $P = P_1 \times P_2 \times P_3 = 10 \times 10 \times 10 = 1000$.
   Note: This makes sense when you also relate the problem to a sequence, beginning with the combinations 0-0-0, 0-0-1, 0-0-2... In ascending order, the last 3-digit combination would be 9-9-9. Although it may seem that there would be 999 possible combinations, you must also include the initial combination: 0-0-0.

48. F: Compute the product using the FOIL method, in which the *First* term, then the *Outer* terms, the *Inner* terms, and finally the *Last* terms are figured in sequence of multiplication. As a result, $(a + b)(a - b) = a^2 + ba - ab - b^2$. Since ab is equal to ba, the middle terms cancel each other out, which leaves $a^2 - b^2$.

49. A: The mode is the number that appears most often in a set of data. If no item appears most often, then the data set has no mode. In this case, Kyle achieved one hit a total of three times, two hits twice, three hits once, and four hits once. One hit occurred the most times, and therefore the mode of the data set is 1.

50. G: The mean, or average, is the sum of the numbers in a data set, divided by the total number of items. This data set contains seven items, one for each day of the week. The total number of hits that Kyle had during the week is the sum of the numbers in the right-hand column, or 14. This gives $Mean = \dfrac{14}{7} = 2$.

51. A: The mean, or average, of the distribution can be computed by multiplying each grade by the number of students obtaining it, summing all products, and then dividing by the total number of students. Here, $n = 4.2$. The median is the value for which an equal number of students have received higher or lower grades. Here, $p = 4$. The mode is the most frequently obtained grade, and here $q = 3$.

52. J: 10% of the tested population of 40 students is 4 students. Four students got grades of 7 or higher.

53. C: If $70, the amount used to buy more lemons, represents 35% of Herbert's earnings, then 1% corresponds to $\dfrac{\$70}{35}=\$2$, and 15% corresponds to $\$2\times15=\$30$.

54. H: To determine this, you must solve the given equation for x. Since $10x+2=7$, we have $x=\dfrac{7-2}{10}=\dfrac{5}{10}=0.5$, and 2$x$ = 1. Alternately, $10x=5$. Divide both sides by 5 to get $2x=1$.

55. B: Zero is the only number that gives the same result when multiplied or divided by a factor. In each case, the answer is zero.

56. K: All of the other capital letters shown are symmetrical with respect to a horizontal axis drawn through the middle, as in the H shown in the figure. Only Z is not symmetrical in this respect.

57. C: She has been working at the rate of 10 papers per hour. She has 30 papers remaining, and must grade them in the 2.5 hours that she has left, which corresponds to a rate of 12 papers per hour. $\dfrac{12}{10}=120\%$ of her previous rate, or 20% faster.

58. J: The ratio of the ruler's height to the distance from eye to ruler, which is the tangent of the angle subtended at the eye by the ruler's height, must be the same as the ratio of the lighthouse's height to its distance, which is the tangent of the same angle. Since 3 inches = ¼ foot, we have $\dfrac{1/4}{2}=\dfrac{60}{D}$, and solving for D gives $D=\dfrac{2\times60}{1/4}=4\times120=480\,\text{feet}$.

59. B: The diagonal of the square corresponds to the diameter of the circle. This allows for calculation of the side a by the Pythagorean Theorem, where the diameter is d = 2r: $d^2=4r^2=a^2+a^2$. Thus, $4r^2=2a^2$, and the area of the square is $a^2=2r^2$.

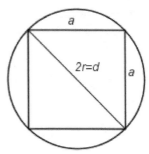

60. J: The sides of a triangle must all be greater than zero. The sum of the lengths of the two shorter sides must be greater than the length of the third side. Since we are looking for the minimum value of the perimeter, assume that the longer of the two given sides, which is 6, is the longest side of the triangle. In this case, the third side must be greater than 6 – 4 = 2. Since we are told that the sides are all integral numbers, the last side must be 3 units in length. Thus, the minimum length for the perimeter is 4 + 6 + 3 = 13 units.

Reading

Number	Answer	Number	Answer
1	C	21	D
2	J	22	G
3	A	23	A
4	K	24	J
5	C	25	E
6	G	26	H
7	B	27	A
8	J	28	K
9	D	29	D
10	K	30	G
11	C	31	C
12	J	32	F
13	B	33	E
14	K	34	H
15	A	35	B
16	J	36	K
17	C	37	B
18	F	38	K
19	E	39	C
20	K	40	J

1. C: In the first sentence the phrase "so long had sleep been denied her" tells us she had been prevented from sleeping for some time.

2. J: The text tells us she was feigning, which means to pretend, to be asleep.

3. A: Despite his ugliness and deformity, Garth is a gentle soul who wants to be accepted as a friend by the girl.

4. K: AT first repelled by the sight of Garth in the window, the girl eventually expresses pity when she learns that he is deaf, too.

5. C: Garth's deformities are repugnant to her at first, and she must overcome this emotion.

6. G: He calls back to her that he is hidden from sight, and his voice is described as plaintive and pained.

7. B: The text tells us that he sees her lips move and assumes she is sending him away, because he cannot hear that she is calling to him.

8. J

9. D: At first she was amazed at the extent of Garth;s deformities, but she has quickly become more sympathetic and has come to pity him

- 136 -

10. K: The girl quickly understands Garth's sadness about his own condition and sympathizes with him.

11. C: An archipelago is a large group or chain of islands.

12. J: The article deals primarily with the ways the colonists fed themselves: their crops and the foods they hunted. While it also describes New Zealand's prehistory, the main focus is on food sources.

13. B: The article states that the islands were colonized by Polynesians in the fifteenth century but that the first settlers had arrived some 400 years earlier than that.

14. K: The passage states that the first settlers were forced to rely on fishing for their food.

15. A: When an increased population had driven a major food source to extinction, they began to fight for control over the remaining food supply.

16. J: The article tells us that coconuts did not grow in New Zealand, and that some of the other crops would grow only on North Island.

17. C: The sweet potato could be stored, providing a source of food during the winter when other food gathering activities were difficult.

18. F: The sweet potato provided a winter food source through storage, allowing the population to increase.

19. E: All of the reasons given are good ones for locating the camps near the source of food production.

20. K: As the human population increased, they depleted many of their food source faster than the populations could reproduce and renew themselves.

21. D: The passage describes the artistry of Greek coinage and gives the reasons why so much effort went into designing them.

22. G: The first sentence shows that the author thinks of coins as utilitarian objects and that few of them are designed in a manner that makes them worth considering as something more than that.

23. A: "Delectation" means to savor or to enjoy the flavor or beauty of something, in this case the design of the coins.

24. J: The word is defined in passing in the text in the second sentence.

25. E: The passage describes the coins as artistic objects, not simply because they were the first coins, but also because of the historical situation which is described, and which led to their being designed with great care and pride.

26. H: The text states that new coins were developed frequently, to commemorate battles, treaties, etc.

27. A: The text tells us that the designers were highly skilled and that they were so proud of their work that they signed it.

28. K: The sentence contrasts the artistic content of the coins with their use as a practical means of commercial exchange.

29. D: The text tells us that coin designs changed along with larger sculptures to reflect changing Greek artistic tastes.

30. G: The frequent need for new designs meant that the artisans who did the work had ample opportunity to perfect their skills.

31. C: The passage describes several distinctive features of annelid anatomy and tells how some of them differ from other worms.

32. F: The term is defined in the text as an organization of the anatomy into segments.

33. E: The term is defined in the text between commas.

34. H: The text gives the example of feet specializing into grasping organs to illustrate this evolutionary advantage of segmental plasticity.

35. B: Nematodes differ from the annelids in the structure of the coelum. Lumbricus and leeches are both members of the Annelida.

36. K: The text gives the example of parapodia modified for grasping to illustrate evolutionary plasticity among metameres.

37. B: The text states that the annelid coelum is formed later during embryology and probably evolved at a later time, as well.

38. K: The text indicates that the cerebral ganglia are enlarged, whereas the remaining ganglia in the nerve cord are merely repeating (unspecialized) units.

39. C: The text defines metemeres as segments, and discusses segmentation as the distinguishing feature of the phylum.

40. J: The paragraph tells us that annelids can live in salt or fresh water and on land, and then gives examples.

Science

Number	Answer	Number	Answer
1	D	21	B
2	J	22	F
3	B	23	A
4	J	24	J
5	B	25	C
6	J	26	G
7	B	27	A
8	J	28	J
9	B	29	B
10	J	30	J
11	B	31	B
12	F	32	H
13	B	33	C
14	F	34	J
15	D	35	D
16	F	36	G
17	C	37	D
18	J	38	J
19	A	39	C
20	H	40	J

1. D: The graph shows that temperatures in the lower stratosphere are -50°C or lower, permitting more efficient engine operation. The text indicates that 75% of the Earth's atmosphere is in the troposphere, which is below the stratosphere. It also states that convective mixing of air, and therefore the effects of weather, are characteristic of the troposphere. In the stratosphere, temperature-based layering of air leads to a stable environment. All of these effects combine to allow jets to operate with the best fuel efficiency possible in the lower stratosphere.

2. J: This can be read from the graph. The thermosphere contains both the coldest and the highest temperatures in the atmospheric regions beneath outer space. In the thermosphere, atmospheric gases form layers of relatively pure molecular species. In its lower reaches, CO_2 contributes to cooling through radiative emission, as in the mesosphere. In its upper reaches, molecular oxygen absorbs solar radiation and causes significant warming.

3. B: The pitch of a sound depends upon the frequency of the sound wave. The higher the frequency, the higher the sound's pitch. Frequency varies inversely with wavelength, so that a higher pitched sound with a higher frequency will have a longer wavelength. The volume of a sound depends upon the degree to which the molecules of air (or any other medium through which the sound travels) are compressed. This compression is represented by the wave amplitude. The greater the amplitude, the louder the sound.

4. J: The waves corresponding to the two emitted sounds will be added, and what will be heard by the observer will be the sum of the two waves. Since these waves are one-half of a wavelength apart, they are perfectly out of phase, and they will cancel one another out. That is, the amplitude peak of one wave will coincide in space with the amplitude trough of the other. This phenomenon is

called cancellation. The opposite is also possible: if the waves were perfectly in phase, they would combine additively, producing a much louder sound. Finally, if the waves were out of phase with one another, this would cause the intensity of the sound to vary.

5. B: The vertical axis of this graph is an exponential scale, with each regularly-spaced tick mark corresponding to a ten-fold increase in the quantity being measured. The curve corresponding to the control cells, those grown in the absence of the drug, shows a cell concentration of approximately 500 cells/mL at the start, 5000 cells/mL after 4 days, and 50,000 cells per mL after 8 days, indicating an exponential growth pattern in which the number of cells increases by a factor of ten every four days.

6. J: The effects of two concentrations of methotrexate (MTX) on the growth of cancer cells are shown by the open pentagons and solid squares in the figure. These growth curves may be compared to the growth of untreated cells (the control) shown by the solid circles. It can be seen that, at a concentration of 10 micromoles per liter (10 micromolar), cell growth is slightly inhibited when compared to the control. At the greater concentration of 100 micromoles per liter (equivalent to 0.1 millimolar), the cells do not grow at all. The experiment is concerned with cancer cells, not bacteria, so choice G is incorrect.

7. B: Sexual reproduction allows the genetic information from two parents to mix. Recombination events between the two parental copies of individual genes may occur, creating new genes. The production of new genes and of new gene combinations leads to an increase in diversity within the population, which is a great advantage in terms of adapting to changes in the environment.

8. J: The charge must be conserved in the reaction. Since the reactants, two helium atoms, each have two protons, they will have a total electric charge of +4. The reaction product, helium-4, also has two protons, and therefore has a total charge of +2. Two positive charges are lacking to balance the reaction. Of the choices given, only K, with two protons, has a charge of +2.

9. B: Since tritium is an isotope of hydrogen, the nucleus contains a single proton, giving it a charge of +1. The extra neutrons do not contribute to the charge. Electrons have a charge of -1. In order to neutralize the single positive charge of the nuclear proton, a single orbiting electron is required.

10. J: Volcanic activity allows molten magma to reach the surface of the Earth, where it cools and solidifies into rock, a process akin to freezing. As the diagram and text both indicate, these types of rocks are known as igneous rocks. Examples of igneous rocks are obsidian and basalt. The type of igneous rock formed depends upon the chemical composition of the magma.

11. B: Metamorphic rocks ("metamorphic" means "changed form") are formed at great depths, usually from sedimentary precursors. As more and more sediment accumulates above them, the increased pressure and heat forces the relatively open crystal structure of the sedimentary rocks to collapse and adopt a denser structure. Examples of metamorphic rocks are quartz and gneiss.

12. F: Evolutionary fitness is a measure of the ability to transmit genes to subsequent generations. As such, it is characterized by the ability to produce offspring. Although the male wolf described in choice A died young, he lived long enough to produce 4 offspring, more than any of the animals described in the other choices. Therefore, his genes have the greatest chance of being passed on. It is important to realize that evolutionary "success," or fitness, simply requires an organism to live long enough to reproduce, and is measured exclusively by reproductive success.

13. B: An allele is a variant of the original DNA sequence for a gene. It may differ from the original by a single base (for example, it may contain a C in place of a G), or by a whole region in which the sequence of bases differ. It may have extra bases in it (insertions) or be missing some material (deletions). Whatever the difference, it will result in RNA, and subsequently a protein, whose sequence differs from that of the original. Sometimes, these differing proteins are defective. They may result in disease or developmental anomalies. Sometimes they are benign, as in the difference between blue and brown eyes in humans.

14. F: The sequence can be read directly from the table. It is read three bases at a time, since three bases constitute a codon and provide the information required to specify a single amino acid. In the sequence given, the first codon is GTT. The table shows that this corresponds to the amino acid valine. Similarly, the second codon is ACA, which corresponds to threonine. The third codon, AAA, corresponds to lysine, and the fourth, AGA, to arginine. Each sequence of amino acids produces a specific protein which is different from any other.

15. D: Begin parsing each sequence from the first base and break it into triplets to represent each codon. The sequence in choice A, for example, is GTA CCC CTA, representing valine-proline-leucine. Only the sequence in choice D contains one of the three STOP codons, which are TGA, TAA, and TAG. In choice D, the second codon is TAA. When the polymerase reaches this codon, it will begin the process of disengaging from the DNA, ending the mRNA copy and ultimately the protein product of the gene.

16. F: The DNA molecule is a long chain of phosphoribose to which bases are attached. The sequence of bases specifies the individual amino acids that are chained together to make a protein. There are 4 different bases and 23 different amino acids. Each amino acid is specified by a three-base "word," called a codon in the language of DNA. As the table shows, the 4 bases can be strung together in 64 different ways to encode the 23 different amino acids (plus STOP signals), so that some amino acids may be specified by more than a single codon.

17. C: While proteins are encoded in the DNA, they are actually produced by ribosomes, which string the proteins together from amino acids in the cell's cytoplasm. The information required to string proteins into the correct sequence is provided by mRNAs that are made by polymerases, which read the codons in the DNA. Transfer RNAs bring the amino acids to the ribosomes, where they are assembled into proteins.

18. J: Phosphoribose provides the backbone of the DNA chain of which genes are comprised. There, bases such as cytosine and guanine are strung together and organized into triplets known as codons, which encode the protein to be made. The protein itself will be assembled far from the gene, which is in the cell's nucleus, by the ribosome, which is in the cytoplasm of the cell.

19. A: The velocities of both the wind and the aircraft can be represented by vectors, with the length of the vector representing the speed and the direction of the vector representing the direction of either the wind or the airplane. Since the wind speed opposes that of the plane, the pilot will measure the sum of the actual wind speed plus that of his aircraft:

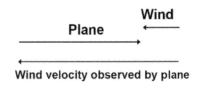

Wind velocity observed by plane

20. H: The chart shows that plastic and cardboard materials both comprise 15% of the collected materials, so it is incorrect to say that there is more plastic than cardboard. They are present in equal quantities.

21. B: Oogenesis is the process that gives rise to the ovum, or egg, in mammals. The oocyte is the immature egg cell in the ovary. In humans, one oocyte matures during each menstrual cycle. It develops first into an intermediate form called the ootid, and eventually into an ovum. The prefix oo- is derived from Greek, and means "egg."

22. F: The reactions described in the text are ones during which negatively charged electrons are produced by a reaction that reduces the positively-charged lead anode. The reducing agent, in turn, is oxidized by this reaction. These electrons travel through the wire to the negatively-charged cathode, where they react with the sulfuric acid oxidizer and reduce it, forming lead sulfate. In a car battery, the anode is the positively-charged electrode, and is normally indicated by a red marking.

23. A: In an oxidation reaction, an oxidizing agent gains electrons from a reducing agent. By contributing electrons, the reducing agent reduces (makes more negative) the charge on the oxidizer. In the car battery, reduction of the positively-charged anode provides electrons, which then flow to the cathode, where an oxidation takes place. In an oxidation, an oxidizing agent increases (makes more positive) the charge on a reducer. In this way, the extra electrons in the negatively charged cathode are neutralized by the surrounding oxidizing agent.

24. J: The reaction described in the text is one during which two water molecules (H_2O) are produced for each lead oxide (PbO_2) molecule that reacts at the cathode.

25. C: The data indicates that up until about 4 weeks, the silk production from both colonies was similar. This suggests that the worms from each colony produced the same amount of silk, and that choices A and B are incorrect. The data does indicate that, over the long term, the silk produced by the entire colony of genetically diverse worms was greater than the silk produced by the entire colony of genetically uniform worms. This might be because the worms produce for a longer time, or because of some other mechanism. The experiment does not indicate what that mechanism might be.

26. G: The increase in productivity from the diverse culture occurs at about 4 weeks, coinciding with the time at which new worms are hatched and begin to produce silk.

27. A: The digestion of starch begins with its exposure to the enzyme amylase, which is present in the saliva. Amylase attacks the glycosidic bonds in starch, cleaving them to release sugars. This is the reason why some starchy foods may taste sweet if they are chewed extensively. Another form of amylase is produced by the pancreas, and continues the digestion of starches in the upper intestine. The di- and tri-saccharides, which are the initial products of this digestion, are eventually converted to glucose, a monosaccharide that is easily absorbed through the intestinal wall.

28. J: The term hydrologic cycle is defined in the first paragraph, where it is described as being equivalent to the water cycle. It is derived from the Greek root hydros, which means "water."

29. B: The second paragraph gives examples of different storage reservoirs for water in the water cycle. Underground aquifers are one of the examples given. An aquifer (a word derived from the Latin root aqua, meaning water) is any geologic formation containing ground water.

30. J: According to the table, the average residence time of water in soil is only two months. Only its residence time in the atmosphere, 9 days, is shorter. Residence time is defined in the text as the average amount of time that a water molecule spends in each of the reservoirs shown in the table before it moves on to the next reservoir of the water cycle.

31. B: According to the final paragraph of the text, ocean levels actually fall during an ice age. This is because more water is stored in ice caps and glaciers when the prevailing temperatures are very cold, so less water remains in the oceans.

32. H: Because the addition of heat causes the molecules of a substance to increase their rate of motion, it is considered a form of kinetic energy. The temperature of a substance is proportional to the kinetic energy of the molecules of which it is made. Addition of heat to a system usually results in an increase in temperature, but temperature is not a form of heat. It is a measure of the amount of kinetic energy present in a system.

33. C: Energy in the form of heat is always absorbed by the molecules of a substance to make them move faster. During a change of state, some molecules are absorbing energy and escaping the solid phase to become liquid, or escaping the liquid phase to become gas. Since molecules in a gas move faster than those in a liquid and molecules in a liquid move faster than those in a gas, the average speed increases. Note that choice E is incorrect since the heat of vaporization for water is greater than its heat of fusion.

34. J: In region B of the graph, the water is at 0°C. Heat is being added to it and it is progressively changing to a liquid. In region C, the temperature is climbing from 0°C to 100°C, and all of the water is in a liquid phase. In region D, the water is at 100°C, and is progressively changing to a gas as more energy is added. Once it has all changed to a gas, the temperature will once again increase as more heat is added (region E).

35. D: Water at 1°C is in the liquid phase. Using the definition of the specific heat capacity given in the text, it will take 99 calories to raise the temperature of 1 gm of liquid water to 100°C. Using the definition of the heat of vaporization given in the text, it will take an additional 540 calories to turn it into the gaseous phase once it reaches 100°C. Finally, an additional calorie must be added to bring the temperature of the gas up to 101°C. Therefore, the total amount of heat which must be added is 640 calories.

36. G: Region B of the graph represents the transition between the solid and liquid phases of water. If heat is added to the system, solid water melts into liquid. Conversely, if heat is removed from the system, liquid water will freeze in this region of the graph. Similarly, region D represents the transition between liquid and gaseous water. In this region, water either evaporates or condenses, depending upon whether heat is added to or removed from it. Sublimation (choice K) is the direct transition from the solid to the gaseous phase, which occurs only under conditions of very low pressure.

37. D: Since the cylinder is airtight, the piston cannot sink into the injected fluids, so it will not displace a volume of fluid equal to its weight. Since liquids are not compressible, the density of the injected fluid makes no difference in this experiment. Equal volumes of any fluid will raise the cylinder by an equal amount.

38. J: The terms accuracy and precision, often used interchangeably in informal speech, have specific meanings as scientific terms. Accuracy describes how close a measurement is to the actual dimension that is being measured. In this case, both measurements have the same accuracy. Precision is the degree of exactness that characterizes a measurement, or the number of significant figures with which it can be reported. Nancy's measurement is the more precise of the two, because she has reported the length to the nearest millimeter, whereas Mark's measurement is to the nearest centimeter. Note that the ruler cannot measure the length to a greater precision than that which Nancy has specified because the millimeter is its smallest division.

39. C: Both cannonballs will be subject to a vertical acceleration due to the force of gravity. Although there is an additional horizontal component to the velocity of cannonball A, its vertical velocity will be the same. In each case, the height of the object at time t seconds will be

$$h = -\frac{1}{2}t^2 + 20$$

.

40. J: First, note that 5 meters equals 500 cm, so the horizontal speed of the cannonball is 500 cm/sec. Momentum must be conserved in the recoiling system. The vertical motion due to gravity can be ignored, since it involves conservation of momentum between the cannonball and the Earth rather than the cannon. In the horizontal dimension, conservation of momentum dictates that $MV = mv$, where M and V represent the mass and the velocity of the cannon, and m and v represent the mass and the velocity of the cannonball. Solving for V gives

$$V = \frac{1}{M} \times mv = \frac{1}{500} \times 5 \times 500 = 5$$

cm/sec.